Benjamin Brogden Orridge

Illustrations of Jack Cade's Rebellion

From Researches in the Guildhall Records

Benjamin Brogden Orridge

Illustrations of Jack Cade's Rebellion
From Researches in the Guildhall Records

ISBN/EAN: 9783337252045

Printed in Europe, USA, Canada, Australia, Japan

Cover: Foto ©ninafisch / pixelio.de

More available books at **www.hansebooks.com**

ILLUSTRATIONS

OF

JACK CADE'S REBELLION,

FROM RESEARCHES IN THE GUILDHALL RECORDS;

TOGETHER WITH

SOME NEWLY-FOUND LETTERS OF LORD BACON, &c.

BY B. BROGDEN ORRIDGE, F.G.S.

TO WHICH ARE ADDED CONTRIBUTIONS BY

W. DURRANT COOPER, F.S.A.,

ON THE RISING OF CADE AND HIS FOLLOWERS IN KENT AND SUSSEX.

LONDON:
JOHN CAMDEN HOTTEN, 74 AND 75, PICCADILLY.
1869.

Price to Subscribers, One Guinea.

TO THE

RIGHT HON. WILLIAM-PAGE BARON HATHERLEY,

LORD HIGH CHANCELLOR OF ENGLAND.

My Lord,

Some thirty-five years ago, Mr. Basil Montagu, in the preface to his "Life of Bacon," recorded his thanks to "his dear friend Mr. William Wood" for "encouragement during the progress of the work," and "for his admirable translation of the Novum Organum."

The University of Oxford marked her approval of that translation, by the use of it on the part of her students.

Your Lordship's appreciation, thus evidenced, of the most illustrious of your predecessors, indeed the very fact of your being the translator alluded to, is I am sure not generally known to your fellow-countrymen. I trust I shall stand excused of presumption if I point to the fact in dedicating this volume to your Lordship.

I have the honour to be,

Your Lordship's obedient servant,

B. BROGDEN ORRIDGE.

PREFACE.

It is perhaps not generally known that Lord Bacon and Robert Cecil (Lord Salisbury) were descended from Jack Cade's London agent. The information in these pages relative to the memorable insurrection under Cade's leadership was only made public for the first time last year. My own researches amongst the Guildhall Records were notified in the Transactions of the London and Middlesex Archæological Society. The labours of Mr. Durrant Cooper, F.S.A., amongst the State Records were inserted in the Transactions of the Archæological Societies of Kent and Sussex.

It appeared to me, that the facts thus acquired merited preservation in a distinct form, and with Mr. Durrant Cooper's assent I determined on reprinting them together.

Why Thomas Cooke, draper, a young citizen from Suffolk, should have been selected as the London agent for a great rebellion we can only conjecture. It was probably due to a native vigour and resolution of character, which won attention at a critical moment, when the services of such a man were specially needed by the Yorkist faction.

Among the descendants of this eminent citizen we find not only such illustrious men as FRANCIS BACON and ROBERT CECIL, but the names also of a multitude of departed worthies who have won a notable position in our national annals. Amongst living men some of these descendants occupy the highest rank in the Peerage; others have made their mark in the House of Commons.

I have printed some letters of Lord Bacon that I found among the correspondence at Guildhall. Two of these letters refer to a claim of King James the First to nominate the Bailiff of Ossulston hundred. I pointed out the existence of these letters to the learned Town Clerk of London, who informed me that no such officer was now appointed by the Corporation, nor had any such appointment been made in his memory. I called the attention of my learned friend Mr. W. H. Black, F.S.A., late Assistant-Keeper of the Public Records, to Lord Bacon's letters on the subject, and he was good enough to favour me with a reply as follows :—

The county of Middlesex was granted to the citizens of London by King John's third Charter, dated 5 July, in his first year, by the name of the "Sheriffwick of London and Middlesex, with all the customs and things to the Sheriffwick belonging, within the city and without, by land and by water, for the annual fee-farm rent of 300*l.* payable half-yearly."

This was not a new grant, but a confirmation of what had been enjoyed "in antient times," and it was made to the citizens and their heirs.

Hence the bailiewick of the hundred, and especially of the hundred of Ossulston, within which the city is locally situate (though not a part thereof), must have been an appurtenance or right of the shrievalty, and the Crown would have no right of appointment. The Crown could only exercise rights over its own demesnes in the county.

See a translation of the Charter in Maitland, i. 74, 75, edit. 1772. I have not the original Latin before me, but I well remember copying the original at Guildhall in 1833.

W. H. BLACK.

It will be observed that Lord Bacon's opinion on this claim is uncalled-for and evasive. It appears as though the mere contact with such a king as James the First was detrimental to the nobler part of Bacon's nature. Lord Macaulay remarks that "the indignation excited by the claims James put forward, and the scorn excited by his concessions, went on growing together. By his fondness for worthless minions, and by the sanction he gave to their tyranny, he kept discontent constantly alive. It was no light thing, that, on the very eve of the decisive struggle between our kings and their parliaments, royalty should be exhibited to the world stammering, slobbering, shedding unmanly tears, trembling at a drawn sword, and talking in the style alternately of a buffoon and of a pedagogue."

As an Englishman, I truly wish that Lord Macaulay had seen the Guildhall letters. Certainly the language of King James the First to the shrewd money-making traders of London, imbued at the time with puritanical feelings, was the extreme of folly, and affords a striking contrast to the strong will and determination of purpose of the great Elizabeth. Writing of her, Robert Cecil said that "she was more than a man, and in truth sometimes less than a woman." It would be extremely interesting to get at the real opinion of this astute minister respecting James the First.

B. B. O.

33, *St. John's Wood Park*,
    October 1st, 1869.

CONTENTS.

PAGE

Neglect of Records of Corporation of London—Lord Bacon—
Robert Cecil—The Bacon Family—Nicholas Bacon, painter
—Richard Bacon, common councilman—Alderman William
Bacon—Alderman James Bacon—Nicholas Bacon, mercer,
1400—Nicholas Bacon, mercer, 1540 and 1562—Philip
Malpas, sheriff 1439, M.P. for London 1441—Returned
for the office of Alderman by Lime Street Ward, 1448—
Rejected by the Court of Aldermen, but ultimately elected
through the interposition of Henry VI.—In 1450 Malpas
removed from his office on the approach of Jack Cade—
Thomas Cooke, warden of the Drapers' Company in 1439,
when they obtained a charter of incorporation—Appointed
Cade's London agent in 1450—Dr. Hook's account of
Jack Cade—Cade admitted into the City by the Common
Council—Alderman Robert Horne committed for opposing
Cade—Horne and Malpas attacked by Cade—Thomas
Cooke married to Philip Malpas's daughter—His son,
Philip Cooke, born in 1461—Malpas captured by Columpne—The pardons of Cade and his followers—The
will of Philip Malpas appoints his son-in-law Sir Ralph
Jocelyn and Thomas Fermory his executors—Allusions
to Thomas Cooke in the will—In 1456 Cooke appointed
alderman of Vintry Ward—Mayor in 1462-3—Made
Knight of the Bath—In 1467 began to build Gidea Hall,
near Romford—Tyranny of Edward IV.—Cooke tried for
high treason and acquitted—In 1469 Cooke reinstated as
alderman—His efforts to obtain redress in 1470—His
character as a member of the House of Commons—
Return of Edward IV.—Cooke's flight—His capture—

CONTENTS

PAGE

The Duke of Buckingham's speech in Guildhall for the Duke of Gloucester—His allusion to Sir Thomas Cooke's wrongs—Cooke's death in 1478—His will—Sir Anthony Cooke, great-grandson of Sir Thomas Cooke—Father of Lady Burghley and Lady Bacon—Appoints Lord Burghley and Sir Nicholas Bacon his executors—Pedigree of the Cooke family . . . . 1 to 23

John Cade's followers in Kent—Their names—Transition of the names of occupations—Errors of Holinshed—Detail of negociations with Cade in St. Margaret's Southwark—Accurate muster lists—Not a disorganized mob: the men being summoned by the Parish Constables—Discontent of the Kentish people—Cade joined by contingents from Sussex, Surrey, and Essex—Complaints of the Commons of Kent—Cade complains of the insufficiency of the pardons—Attacks Queenborough Castle unsuccessfully—The King's proclamation—Offers a reward for capturing Cade—Alexander Iden, sheriff of Kent, and others capture Cade—On 15th July, 1450, Iden and his aiders brought the dead body of Cade to the Council—Their reward by the King—Iden rewarded for capturing Robert Spence—List of goods taken from Cade and sold by the King—Malpas purchases goods of which he had been robbed—Green box labelled "Cade otherwise Mortimer"—Punishment of Cade's adherents—The name of Cade—In 1452 (two years afterwards) a further act of attainder passed—Robert Poynings, Cade's carver and sewer—Writ in 1456 to seize Poynings' possessions and those of his brother and friends . . . . 24 to 78

The part taken by Sussex in Cade's rising—Musters levied by constables—Murder of the bishop—Landing of the French—Unpopularity of Lord Say and Sele—The Abbot of Battle and the Prior of Lewes sanction the movement—Cade enters London—Commission of Oyer and Terminer—Trials for treason at Guildhall—Execution of Lord de Saye—Fight with the citizens: Mathew Gouche and

Alderman Sutton killed—Recital of Cade's pardon—He is therein called "John Mortimer"—Names of Sussex followers .   .   .   .   71 to 82

Appendix—Mr. Francis Bacon to the Lord Mayor—Sir Francis Bacon and Sir Henry Yelverton to the Lord Mayor—Sir Francis Bacon to the Lord Mayor—The same to the same—The same to the same—Lord Bacon to the Lord Mayor—The same to the same—Lord Bacon and others to the Lord Mayor—Alderman Sir Ralph Jocelyn, K.B.—Lord Bacon's arms and extract from will—Connection of Lord Bacon's family with the Corporation of London—Sir Anthony Cooke—Mildred Lady Burghley—Lady Bacon—Lady Russell—Lady Killigrew—Lady Rowlett—Fabyan's character of Sir Thomas Cooke—Ben Jonson's character of Lord Bacon—"The Times" on the Marquis of Salisbury—Monument to William Cooke in the church of St. Martin-in-the-Fields .   .   .   83 to 97

ALDERMAN PHILIP MALPAS

AND

ALDERMAN SIR THOMAS COOKE, K.B.

THE archives of the little town of Stratford-on-Avon have been closely scrutinized with the view of eliciting any circumstance that is linked with the name, or has a bearing on the family connections, of Shakespeare. But it is doubtful whether the records of the Corporation of London have ever been examined with the same energetic interest in reference to either of Shakespeare's great contemporaries, the illustrious author of *Inductive Science*, or his cousin, the renowned statesman Robert Cecil.

The name of Bacon is one of great antiquity in the city of London, and frequently occurs in many of the most ancient of the records belonging to the Corporation. Among others, in 1284, we find that Nicholas Bacon, painter, acknowledged that he was bound to Hugh Motun, City Chamberlain, in the sum of twenty shillings for ciniple, vermilion, canvas, varnish and verdigris;* and in 1347 Richard Bacon served as one of the Common Council for Bridge Ward. I have also found among them the election of William Bacon as Alderman of Coleman Street Ward in 1479,† and of James Bacon (the brother of the Lord Keeper) on the 22nd April, 9th Elizabeth, when the inhabitants of Aldersgate Ward, having (in the place of Lionel Duckett) nomi-

---

* Mr. Riley, in *Memorials of London and London Life*, remarks that there is probably no earlier passage in existence having reference to varnish painting on canvas.

† Corporation Records, Journal 8, fol. 232 b.

nated James Bacon, fishmonger,* William Dane, ironmonger, Francis Barnham,† draper, and Thomas Keighley, leatherseller, "the said James Bacon was elected and duly sworn in for the execution of his said office."

Mr. Foss remarks of Sir Nicholas Bacon, the Lord Keeper, that "he could claim respectable, but by no means opulent, parentage."

"There can be little doubt that the two judges, John and Thomas Bacon, noticed under the reigns of Edward II. and III. came from the same stock.‡"

In the records of the Mercers' Company I found that in the year 1400 Nicholas Bacon was one of the wardens, in 1540 and 1562 another Nicholas Bacon filled the office.

My principal desire, however, is to invite the attention of the reader to some particulars relating to the two eminent citizens and aldermen of London who were the progenitors not only of Francis Bacon and of Robert Cecil, but also of many other distinguished persons.

Philip Malpas and Thomas Cooke lived in times of great political strife, and it would seem entertained widely different political opinions: both witnessed the commencement of the fatal contentions between the rival houses of York and Lancaster, and one certainly lived through the severest part of the national commotion, but both were the victims of gross wrong and oppression.

PHILIP MALPAS, draper, was Sheriff of London in 1439-40, and represented the City in the Parliament of 1441. A search made by me in the civic archives has disclosed some curious facts relative to his election as an alderman. On the 26th February, 1448 (26th Henry VI.), the commonalty of the Ward of Lime Street presented four persons to the Court of Aldermen, viz.: Philip Malpas, Thomas Beaumond, William Dere, and Christo-

---

* Alderman Bacon was sheriff in 1568. His third wife was a daughter of Humphrey Packington, and widow of Alderman Jackman, Sheriff 1564.

† A marginal note to the Preface of the third edition of Stowe speaks of the Barnhams as father and son. Francis Barnham was therefore grandfather of Lady Bacon.

‡ *Lives of the Judges*, vol. v. p. 447.

pher Warter, for one of them, according to the custom of the time, to be chosen alderman of that ward; but the nomination was rejected, because the Court of Aldermen affirmed that they were all unfit for the office!* It may be inferred from this decision that the majority of the Court of Aldermen were, even at that early period, opposed to the Lancastrian interests, and desired to exclude Malpas from their body. If it were so, their opposition to him was for the time rendered nugatory by the personal intervention of the King; for on the 1st of April following, it is recorded, that, " on contemplation of divers Royal Letters upon the fitness and special recommendation of the person of the said Philip Malpas to the Mayor and Aldermen directed, the same Philip Malpas was elected by them as Alderman of the said ward, and sworn, as is meet," † &c.; but the following salvo is added to the entry, viz.: " So that this admission of the aforesaid Alderman be in no wise held as an example to expel the Mayor and Aldermen for the time being in future from the liberty to elect any Alderman whomsoever," &c.

I find also the following curious fact noted in the Corporation Records:—" At a Common Council, held the 26th June, 1450, a petition was presented from the commonalty that Philip Malpas should be exonerated from his office of alderman, and the request of the petitioners was conceded to them."‡ The solution of this riddle may be found in the fact of the rising of the Commons of Kent under Jack Cade, his approach to London, and the absence of Henry VI. at Kenilworth. Of course the Court of Common Council had no right to dismiss an alderman; and the expulsion of Malpas was one of those violent party assumptions that always attend civil war. It is in connection with this outbreak that we meet with the name of Thomas Cooke, draper, *as the London agent of Cade.*

It may be assumed that Cooke had previously attained a position of some influence and note in the City, and carried on the business of a draper; for he was one of the four wardens of the Drapers' Company in 1439, when they obtained a Charter of

* Corporation Records, Journal 4, fol. 208 b.   † *Ibid.* fol. 213 b.
‡ Journal, v. fol. 38 b.

Incorporation from Henry VI., and a Grant of Arms from Garter King of Arms.

In Dr. Hook's *Lives of the Archbishops of Canterbury*,* Cade is described as an unknown Irishman, who, in order to give a political significance to the insurrection, assumed to be Sir John Mortimer, brother to the Earl of March.† His bearing, it is said, was princely, and to a commanding figure he added "a pregnant wit." He had served in the French wars, and was well qualified to act the part of a demagogue. The main object of the insurrection (Dr. Hook says) was not a change of dynasty, but to effect such a change of ministry as would place the Court under the control of the Yorkists.‡ "Jack Cade encamped on Blackheath, between Eltham and Greenwich, on the 1st of June, 1450. Here, while he maintained his people by pillaging the country, he opened a communication with the City, styling himself the Captain of the Commons. All business was transacted in an orderly manner. Passports were duly signed, and Thomas Cooke, of London, draper, was constituted the captain's agent. He was required to tax the foreigners—the Genoese, Venetian, and Florentine merchants. They were to be duly convened, and were required to supply 'us, the Captain,' with 12 harnesses of the best fashion, 24 brigandines, 12 battle-axes, 12 glades, 6 horses with saddle and bridle completely harnessed, and a thousand marks in ready money. That the demand was met is inferred by Stowe from the fact that when the rebels entered the city no foreigner was molested." The documentary proofs of these facts are to be found in Holinshed's Chronicles.§

We are told by the Chronicler that Cade and his followers were admitted into the City with the concurrence of the Court of

---

* Vol. v. p. 162.

† The name of Cade was common in the subsidies of Mayfield, Sussex, near Lord Dacre's residence, from the 13th to the 16th century.

‡ *Hook's Lives of the Archbishops of Canterbury*, pp. 163—165. The learned Dean of Chichester, however, was not aware of the attempt to exclude from the office of Alderman a man who, as Member for London, had probably in the House of Commons adhered to the King's interests, or of other significant facts that look as if a mere change of ministry was not alone intended.

§ Vol. iii. pp. 220, 221.

Common Council, who were too much divided to withstand him. According to Fabyan—" Vpon the seconde day of the sayd moneth,* the mayer called a comon counsayll at ye Guyldhall, for to puruey ye withstandynge of thyse rebellys, and other matyers, in which assemble were dyuers opynyons, so that some thought good that the sayd rebellys should be receyued into ye cytie, & some otherwise; amonge ye which, Robert Horne, stokfysshmonger, than beyng an aldermā, spake sore agayne theym that wold haue hym entre. For the whiche sayinges, the comons were so amouyd agayne hym, that they ceasyd nat tyll they hadde hym cōmytted to warde."†

We have seen that Malpas was expelled from the Court of Aldermen by the Common Council on the 26th June. We are told by Fabyan that Alderman Horne was committed by another court on the 2nd of July, and we find these two eminent members of the Lancastrian party were selected by Cade for attack on the second day after his entrance into the city. That he or his followers committed several murderous acts, and made free with the property of the citizens, cannot be doubted.‡

Fabyan's account is, that he " went into the house of Philip Malpas, draper and alderman, and robbed and spoiled his house, and took thence a great substance; but he was forewarned, and thereby conveyed much of his money and plate, or else he had been undone. At which spoylyng were present many poore " " redy to do harme."

Whether Malpas owed this friendly warning to Thomas Cooke does not appear, but one thing is certain, that very shortly afterwards the daughter of Malpas is known to have been the wife of Cooke, and that her son, who was named, after her father, Philip, was born in 1454, the year after Cooke's shrievalty.

The next trace we have of Alderman Malpas is in the year 1461, when, notwithstanding that the battle fought at St. Alban's

---

* July 1450.

† *Chronicle*, p. 623.

‡ Whether Cade was unable to control his followers, or unable to control himself, may be doubtful. It seems clear that his friends in the Corporation were soon opposed to him.

left the Lancastrian party victorious, the young Duke of York, being favourably received by the Londoners, assumed the regal authority as Edward IV. During this state of insecurity (according to Fabyan, p. 638) " dyuers cytezyns auoydyd the cytie and lande, among the whiche Phylyp Malpas, whiche, as before is shewyd," " was robbyd of Jacke Cade, whiche Malpas and others was mette vpon the see with a Frensheman namyd Columpne, and of hyme taken prysoner, and after payed iiij thousand marke for his ransom." The important researches of Mr. W. Durrant Cooper, F.S.A., clearly exhibit the fact that the insurgent body of which Cade was the leader partook very much of the character of a duly authorised army. The musters were levied by the constables in many of the hundreds, and the insurgents included a great number of the gentry and yeomen of Kent, Sussex, and Surrey; the Abbot of Battle, the Prior of Lewes, and a few other ecclesiastics. Mr. Cooper points out that the House of Commons (in 1439) had previously called the attention of the Government to the murders, rapes, robberies, and burnings that were causing discontent among the people in certain districts.

The fact of the house of Philip Malpas being ransacked by Cade seems unquestionable; and indeed, from a record preserved in the Treasury of the Exchequer, Mr. Cooper proves that Malpas actually obtained again *by purchase* from the Treasury some of the goods seized in his house by Cade.

The evidence adduced by Mr. Cooper clearly demonstrates the inaccuracy of Holinshed. It is not true that the men deserted their leaders as soon as shown their pardon. On the morning after the indecisive engagement on London Bridge (6th July) negociations were opened with Cade in the church of St. Margaret, Southwark,* for " a charter of pardon from the King *for them all;*" Cade, as a preliminary, insisting on and obtaining the acceptance by the Chancellor and Bishop Waynfleet of the Bill of Petitions which had been refused by the Privy Council. In his own pardon, which is dated the same day (Monday) as the negociations, Cade is designated John Mortimer. Mr. Cooper remarks : " If Cade had

* For a detailed account of these negociations see the *Chronicles of William of Wyrcester,* p. 76 et seq.

been the low-born person he has been represented, no act of attainder would have been of any operation against his lands and tenements, nor would it have been of importance to declare his blood corrupt."

It is abundantly clear that when "Thomas Cooke of London, draper," was appointed the London agent of John Cade and his associates * he really assumed a most difficult and important task, which could hardly have been offered to any man unless he had great influence, ability, and judgment.

We may infer, from the date of his will and the time when probate was granted, that Malpas died either the latter end of April or the beginning of May 1469.

By his will,† dated 26th April in that year, he describes himself as Philip Malpas, merchant, citizen and draper, of the city of London, &c. After the usual bequest of soul to Almighty God, the blessed Virgin, &c., he desires his body to be buried in the parish church of the Holy Apostle St. Andrew, upon Cornhill,‡ of which parish he describes himself a parishioner. To the high altar of the same church he leaves for offerings forgotten, &c. 20s.; and to the body of the same church for his burial there, &c., 10 marks. He also wills that a priest be provided to read and sing divine service daily in the said church for two years next ensuing after his decease, for his soul, the soul of Julian his late wife, and the souls of their fathers and mothers, and Philippa his daughter, late the wife of Sir Ralph Jocelyn, Knt., &c. He also bequeaths to each of the poor householders in the parish of St. Andrew 6s. 8d. to pray for his soul, and to the most needful poor people of the said parish, every week for five years next after his decease, 6d.; and every year for five years after his decease, he directs wood and coal to the value of 100s. to be purchased and distributed among the poor of the said parish; and to every poor householder of the said parish of St. Andrew, once every year for five years, 2s. to pray for his soul. To the Prioress

---

* Edward Poynings, the uncle of the Countess of Northumberland, was Cade's carver and sewer.
† Prerog. Reg. 27 Godyn.
‡ Now known as St. Andrew Undershaft, Leadenhall Street.

of St. Helen's he bequeaths 20s.; and to "Dame Alice Woodhows," nun there, 20s., and also to every other nun professed in the same house 6s. 8d. to pray for his soul. To relieving the poor people in the Hospital of " Bedelem " without Bishopsgate he bequeaths 100s. &c.; also 5 marks for making a window of glass in the church of the priory of St. Mary Spittal, "late brent;"* and 100s. to be bestowed in linen and woollen clothes for the poor people in the same spittal. To the repair of the highway without Bishopsgate 5 marks, and the highway without Aldgate 100s. To the poor people in the lazar houses of the " loke "† at Kingsland and St. Giles without London, to each house he bequeaths 40s.; and to the poor almspeople of his craft or fellowship of Drapers, being in their almshouses, yearly, during five years next after his decease, 40s. To his brethren the Commonality and Fellowship of the same craft he bequeaths "a stonding cup coūed of silů and gilt." To the reparation of Rochester Bridge 40s. And every year for five years, in bread to the poor prisoners in Newgate, Ludgate, the King's Bench, and Marshalsea, he bequeathed 25l. He also leaves yearly for five years 400 shirts and smocks, 40 pairs of sheets, and 150 gowns of frise to be distributed among the most needful poor people in and about the city of London. To the marriage of poor damsels in the city of London, " of good name and fame," 20 marks yearly for a term of five years, to be distributed as 40s. to each. He also bequeaths 20 marks yearly for five years to making of highways where most needed; and 6s. 8d. each to 500 poor householders in London, to pray for his soul. He also desires that there be found of his goods a priest, " a good honest man, graduat in Scoles," to go about for a year to preach the Word of God devoutly to the people, exhorting them to pray for his soul, &c., and for his salary to have 20 marks, &c. He also bequeaths 20s. yearly to be prayed for at St. Mary Spittal, the three preaching days in Easter week, during twenty years next after his decease; and he further desires his soul to be prayed for every Sunday at Paul's Cross during a term of ten years. To Elizabeth his daughter, the wife of Sir Thomas Cooke, Knt., he bequeaths 500 marks of the 1000 marks, 100l., and 30l., of

* Burnt. † Lock.

"ferme," which the said Sir Thomas was indebted to him, &c.;
and to each of the four sons of said Sir Thomas and Elizabeth
be bequeaths 100 marks more of the said amount owing him,
each to have his part when he arrived at the age of twenty-one
years, with provision for remainder in event of their respective
decease. Then follows a very curious passage, which I give
verbatim:—

"Also where as it hath been demed and surmysed by the said
sir Thomas Cooke heretofore þat I the said Philip Malpas was
the cause of tarying and taking of the goodes of the said sir
Thomas Cooke, which were takin in a Ship which I was in
vppon the see, whan I last passed oũer the see, I the said Philip
Malpas, for myn acquitall and discharge in that behalf, say and
declare verely vpon my conscience þat I was never the cause of
suche said tarying or taking of the said Ship and goodes of the
said sir Thomᵃs Cooke therin, and that the same Ship with
goodes was never so taried nor takyn in my cause or defaute, as
I woll answer vnto God."

This no doubt refers to the matter mentioned by Fabyan, and
quoted in p. 6, in which it appears Malpas was taken prisoner
by a Frenchman named Columpne.

But, to proceed with the will, he bequeaths to "Maister John
Chambre," clerk, 10*l.*; to "Robert Chambre," 20*l.*; and to
Thomas Ram, whom he describes as his "suster's doughter's
sonne," he bequeaths 46*l.* 13*s.* 4*d.*; and to each of the three
sisters of the said Thomas Ram on their marriage he leaves 60*l.* &c.
To Robert Brykkesworth, his servant, 40*l.* and one of his best
"bourd" clothes, one of his best towells, and 100 marks of the
best debts that are owing to him. He also bequeaths to John
Brandon his servant 20 marks; to John Cary, his servant, 10
marks; to "Johanne" his servant 40 marks; and to Elizabeth
his other servant 20*l.*; and to each of the same Johanne and
Elizabeth so much of his best "silũ wessell" as will amount
to 10*l.*; and to the same Johanne and Elizabeth, to be evenly
divided between them, all his "beddyng and napery," and other
clothes of his household linen and woollen, &c. except such parcels thereof as his executors should like to divide between the said

Robert Brikkesworth and Thomas Ram "oute of" his "grete
standard chiste, beyng in" his "grete chambre, and except" his
"gownes and the ffedder bed of" his "bed in the said grete
chambr, and the grete matras thereof, with coullit, celour, testo^r,
and curteyns of the same bed, and the crosters hanging aboute
the same chambr, with the Standard bed and Standard chest for
the said Chambr þat nowe ther stonde, willing alle the same stuf
shall remayne and belef to the said place; the said Johanne to
have first choice of such goods. To Thomas Michell his child
he bequeaths 10 marks, to be delivered to him when of the age
of 21 years, &c. To "Thomas Alyn'" his cook 10 marks, and
"alle the Vessell and necessaries longing to" his "Kytchyn, of
peautre and bras, Iren, treen, and stonen remeveable." Of his
gownes furred and lined he desires John Brikkesworth to have
two thirds, and the remaining third part to be sold, and the
money received for same to be expended for the good of his soul.
"To Kaþyn" the daughter of William Denton, to her marriage,
he bequeaths 5 marks; and to John Foster and Johanne
his wife, to either of them, "a cup of siluer coued," &c.; and to
"maister Thomas Eboralle"* he bequeaths 10*l.* and "a cup
coued of silu and gilt, and a potell potte of siluer." To John
Lucy, haberdasher, dwelling in "Powles Chirchawe," he bequeaths 5*l.*; to Thomas Marsburgh, bowyer, 20*s.*; John Bird,
chaundler, 20*s.*; and Thomas, servaunt with "maister Adam,"
6*s.* 8*d.* He further desires that . . . . Compton, of "Brkynsfeld,"
a poor blind man, have 10*s.* yearly for life. To Sir Ralph Jocelyn,
knt. he bequeaths 100 marks; and to Thomas Fermory, 20*l.*
The residue of all his goods, debts, &c. after all his debts paid
and his will fulfilled, to be disposed in deeds of alms and charity
for his soul, &c.; and he makes and ordains Sir Ralph Jocelyn
and Thomas Fermory his executors.

To James Smith, fishmonger, and Johanne his wife, the sister
of the before-mentioned Thomas Ram, he bequeaths and grants
an annual rent of 40s. for term of their lives, out of a shop situate
in Bridge Street, in the parish of St. Magnus, &c. To Sir

---

* Thomas Eboralle was a priest, being mentioned as such in the early part of
the will.

Thomas Cooke and Elizabeth his wife he bequeaths all his great place in which he was then dwelling, &c., situate in Cornhill and Lime Street in the parish of St. Andrew Cornhill, &c., &c. He also bequeaths to the said Thomas and Elizabeth all his lands and tenements in the parish of St. Andrew Eastcheap; his shop in Bridge Street, in the parish of St. Magnus; and all his lands and tenements, &c. in the parishes of St. Olave and St. Mary Magdalen, in Southwark; to have and to hold to them, and the heirs of their bodies, &c.; provided always, that in case the heir of John Tychborne will buy and have those lands and tenements in Southwark, &c., and that he will pay for the same, &c. 100*l.*, then the said heir of John Tychborne, on payment of said 100*l.*, to have again the same lands, &c. To John Foster and Johanne his wife (the daughter of Sir Thomas and Elizabeth Cooke) he bequeaths all that his tenement called the "Cok," lying in and on the north side of Cornhill, in the parish of St. Peter, and in ward of Lime Street, with remainder in default of heirs, &c. He also wills that the said Sir Ralph Jocelyn, knt., have and hold for his life the manor of "Chaldewell," in the county of Essex, &c., and after the decease of Sir Ralph the said manor to remain to Sir Thomas and Elizabeth Cooke for term of their lives, and after their decease to remain to Philip their son and his heirs, &c., with provisions for remainder in default of heirs, &c. He also bequeaths to Sir Thomas and Elizabeth Cooke, for term of their lives respectively, his place called "Belle hous," and the place called "Appultons," "Porters' ffee," and "Boyeles," in the county of Essex, with all his meadows, &c. at Stratford Langthorn, which he had before assigned and delivered to the said Sir Thomas Cooke, the same to remain after the decease of said Sir Thomas Cooke and Elizabeth his wife unto Thomas, William, and John, their sons, each taking his third part, &c., &c.

This will was proved at Lambeth, the 8th day of May, 1469.

Returning to THOMAS COOKE, it appears that in 1453 (five years after Malpas became alderman, and three years after Jack Cade's rebellion), he was elected as Sheriff; three years later he was chosen as Alderman of the Ward of Vintry; and in the year 1462-3 he filled the office of Lord Mayor. At the time of the coronation of Elizabeth, Queen of Edward IV., in May 1465, Cooke was created a knight of the Bath, and the same honour was also conferred upon the then Lord Mayor, Ralph Jocelyn (brother-in-law to Cooke and ancestor of the Earl of Roden), and some other citizens. Sir Thomas Cooke was evidently a man of considerable wealth, and in high favour at Court. In 1467 he began to build a mansion called Gidea Hall, near Romford in Essex, and obtained a licence for fortifying and embattling it; but on account of his subsequent misfortunes he completed only the front, the remainder being built by one of his descendants.*

The tyranny exercised by Edward IV. against those persons whose riches held out a temptation to visit them with the suspicion of a connection with the House of Lancaster is the subject of severe reprehension by the old historians, and Sir Thomas Cooke was a notable victim.

In 1467 he was impeached of high treason, at the instance of one Hawkins, who, having some years previously requested a loan of him of one thousand marks, upon good security, Sir Thomas answered that he would first know for whom it was and for what intent; when, understanding it was for the use of Queen Margaret (wife of Henry VI.), he told Hawkins that he had no goods that he could convert into money without too much loss, and refused to lend even a hundred pounds; but at the request of the Lady Margaret, sister to the King, he was admitted to bail. No sooner, however, had that royal lady left England, to be married to Charles Duke of Burgundy, than Cooke was again arrested, and sent to the Tower, his effects seized by Lord Rivers, the Queen's father, then Treasurer of England, and his wife committed to the custody of the then Mayor. Sir Thomas was shortly after tried at Guildhall and acquitted. But on his acquittal he was sent to the Bread Street Compter, and from thence to the King's Bench, and was there kept until he paid £8,000 to the King and £800 to the Queen.

His wife, on regaining possession of his house after acquittal, "found it in very evil plight, for the servants of Lord Rivers

* Lysons's *Environs*, vol. iv. p. 186.

and of Sir John Fagge (then Under-Treasurer), had made havoc of what they listed. Also at Gidea Hall, Essex, they had destroyed the deer in his park, his conies and fish, and spared not brass, pewter, bedding, nor all they could carry away; for which never a penny was gotten back in recompense."*

It is stated by Fabyan and the other chroniclers that Lord Rivers and his wife the Duchess of Bedford obtained the dismissal of Chief Justice Markham from his office, for having determined that Cooke was not guilty of treason.

The City Records show that, on the 21st November, 1468, Sir Thomas Cooke was discharged from the office of alderman, on the King's mandate, and that he was reinstated in October of the following year.

On the temporary restoration of Henry VI., in a Parliament which met on the 26th of November, 1470, and of which he appears to have been a member, Cooke "put in a byll into the comon house to be restoryd of the lord Ryuers, and other occacioners of his trouble," lands to the sum of 22,000 marks, of "whiche he had good comfort to haue ben allowyd of King Henry if he had prosperyd."† "And the rather" (adds the chronicler) "for y^t he was of the cōmon house, and therewith a man of great boldnesse of speke and well spoken, and syngulerly wytted and well reasoned."‡ As King Henry's restored rule was but of short duration, it is clear this appeal met with no success.

In the beginning of the following year, 1471, "the mayer" (Sir John Stockton) "ferynge the retourne of kynge Edwarde, fayn hym syke, and so kept his house a great season, all which tyme sir Thomas Cooke, whiche thenne was admytted to his former rome, was sette in his place, and allowyed for his deputie, whiche tourned after to his great trouble and sorowe."§ Edward *did* return

* There is a feminine ring about this passage that makes one fancy the language that of Lady Cooke herself.
† Fabyan's *Chronicle*, p. 660.
‡ The early and the modern historians appear to have been alike appalled by the fact that there has never been any but a very imperfect index to the Guildhall papers. I rejoice to say that I carried an inquiry on this subject in the Court of Common Council, and I believe very important information will be, as a consequence, obtainable on the report of the Committee.
§ Fabyan's *Chronicle*, p. 660.

and resumed possession of the throne in the month of April, and Sir Thomas Cooke, attempting flight by leaving this country for France, was taken by a ship of Flanders, and his son and heir with him, and so set there in prison many days, and lastly was delivered up to King Edward. It is also said that the goods of Sir Thomas Cooke were again seized, and his wife put forth, and commanded to be kept at the mayor's.* How long this state of things lasted, and what events happened to Cooke subsequently, I have not been able to trace; but it is clear from the amount of property he died possessed of, that, though he may have been heavily fined, he was not reduced to poverty. When upon the death of Edward IV. Richard Duke of Gloucester made known his ambitious designs upon the throne, we are told that the Duke of Buckingham was sent into the city to deliver an oration to the assembled citizens in their Guildhall, in order to incite them to favour Richard's projects. In this speech Buckingham dwelt on topics which he knew would come home to the feelings of those whom he was addressing, and amongst other subjects he spoke with much force of the injuries which Sir Thomas Cooke had sustained at the hands of the late King. The following extract from the account handed to us of the duke's speech on this subject may not be deemed uninteresting: "What Cooke," he exclaims, "your owne worshipful neighbour, alderman, and maior of this noble citie! who is of you so either negligent that he knoweth not, or so forgetful that he remembreth not, or so hard-hearted that he pittieth not that worshipful man's losse? What speake we of losse? His vtter spoile and vndeserued destruction, *onelie for that it hapned those to fauour him whome the prince fauoured not.*†

* Fabyan's *Chronicle*, p. 662.

† Does this point to any special friendship with the Earl of Warwick (the king-maker)? A modern writer expresses his surprise at the influence the earl exercised in the City. May not this have been through Sir Thomas Cooke? Had Warwick anything to do with Cooke's negociations with Jack Cade? We know that when Warwick quarrelled with Edward IV. and brought back Henry VI. Cooke was made acting Lord Mayor. It is probable that if the Corporation decide upon a careful scrutiny of the City archives many interesting facts relative to the History of England during the Wars of the Roses will be brought to light. I sincerely hope that the attention of Mr. H. T. Riley may be directed to this subject.

We need not (I suppose) to rehearse of these anie mo by name, sith there be (I doubt not) manie heere present, that either in themselues or in their nigh friends haue knowne as well their goods as their persons greatlie indangered either by feigued quarels or small matters aggreeued with heinous names. And also there was no crime so great of which there could lack a pretext. For sith the king, preuenting the time of his inheritance, atteined the crown by battell, it sufficed in a rich man for a pretext of treason to haue beene of kinred, or aliance, neer familiaritie, or legier acquaintance with any of those who were at anie time the king's enimies, which was at one time or other more than halfe the relme. Thus were neither your goods in suretie, and yet they brought your bodies in ieopardie."[*]

Sir Thomas Cooke died in 1478. By his testament and last will[†] dated the 15th April 1478, after the preliminary bequest of soul to God, &c. &c., he desires his body "to be buried w'in the Churche of the ffreres Augustynes, sett w'in Bradstrete Warde of londoñ, on the south side bitwene the two pillers in the thirde vpmost Arche of stone exopposite the grave and monument of William Edward, Aldreman, late mayre and grocer of london;" and for his tomb to be made of stone he bequeaths 20 marks. He also desires 16 poor men to attend his burial with 12 torches and 4 great tapers of wax, but without "any manner of curious hers or Candlesticks," and each of the said poor men to have 20d. and a "gown clothe of blake frise or lynyng;" he also instructs his executors to desire and pray the mayor and aldermen to be at his burial and month's mind, and describes himself as a parishioner of the parish of St. Peter le Poer, to the altar of which parish church he bequeaths 13s. 4d. for duties forgotten, &c., and to the repair of the body of same church 10s. To each of the four orders of Friars in London, viz., Augustines, Minors, and the Black and White Friars, to say "Placebo and Dirige" within the church of the Augustin Friars on day of his burial, to each order 20s. To the Friars of Chelmsford, Maldon, and every order of Friars of Colchester, 20s. to each order, to sing "Placebo

---

[*] Holinshed's *Chronicle*, vol. iii. p. 391.
[†] Prerog. Reg. 36 Wattis.

and Dirige by note " the day of his burial and month's mind, and three days next after the same, and also on the morning following mass of Requiem by note. To the Grey Friars of Ailesbury 40s., on condition that they keep an obit yearly for 20 years in their church for his soul, the soul of John Maldy, William Thurston, and all christian souls. He also bequeaths 10l. for prayers to be said every Sunday at St. Paul's Cross in London, yearly for a space of six years; also 3l. for prayers to be said at St. Mary Spittal, the three preaching days in Easter week, for a term of 20 years next ensuing his decease; then follows a bequest of 6s. every month for a term of five years next after his decease, to be bestowed in bread among the poor prisoners of Newgate, Marshalsea and King's Bench, to pray for his soul and the soul of Thomas Bassett, &c., and 5 marks to such person or persons as the Prioress and nuns of St. Helen's within Bishopsgate are indebted to, on condition that the said Prioress and convent on the day of his decease and month's mind, within their church, sing " Placebo and Dirige," &c. for his soul, &c. To Sympkin Ludbroke of London, draper, he bequeaths 5 marks, and to his chaplain Sir Robert . . . . . . 4 marks. He also bequeaths to William Taillour his servant 4 marks. To Robert Whittingham his servant 40s., and to John Vale his servant 50l. of the best debts owing to him, &c. He also bequeaths to six poor men such as should be blind and lame and not dwelling in his "rentę in the blak Ale," for a term of 90 years next ensuing after his decease, every Sunday 1d. each, and also that the said poor men and others after them in their stead, each of them to have "bi himself an hous bi the grounde nexte the streete of tho" his "rentę and tenementę sett in blak Alee a foresaide, in the pish of Allhallowes in the Walle in Bradstrete Warde of London a foresaide," to have and to hold the said six tenements during their lives without any rent or charge, and he further desires this bequest to take effect the Sunday eight weeks after his month's mind, &c., and he desires Thomas of Kente and Godfrey, late his servants, to have the preferment or choice of the said six houses, and to the said Thomas he bequeaths 20s. His manual book, and all his mass books, bibles, portuses, saulters, vestments, chalices, corporales, sepultures, altar cloths, and curtains, he desires to remain in the custody of Philip his son, to the intent that he deliver them to John or William his brothers, or either of them who shall happen to be a priest, without any delay the day next before he shall sing his first mass. After his burial and all his debts paid, he bequeaths the residue of all his goods, &c. &c., whatsoever, to be divided into three equal parts. The first part to Elizabeth his wife, the other part to Philip his son, and the third part to be equally divided between John and William his sons, when they arrive at the age of 24 years, &c. &c., with a provision for remainder in event of John and William being priests or dying without issue. To Thomas Rotherham, Lord Chancellor and Bishop of Lincoln, he bequeaths his best "standing Cupp coūed gilt;" and to William Edward, Alderman, to be one of his executors, 10 marks. He also bequeaths 10 marks each to John Vavasour of the Temple, gentleman, and John Hawe* of London, gentleman, and he makes and ordains his son Philip, William Edward, John Vavasour, John Hawe, and Humfrey Howarden, his executors, the last mentioned also to have 10 marks; and for their overseer he appoints the said Lord Chancellor. He then directs his executors after his decease to grant to the Prior and convent of the Augustin Friars an annuity of 40s. yearly of the issues of the place in which he was then dwelling, and of all his other tenements in the parish of St. Peter le Poer, to have and to hold the same from the day of his decease for a term of 90 years; that the said prior and convent, &c., suffer his grave and tomb to be made within their said church, and so to remain for ever, the said prior and convent keeping and observing an obit for his soul, &c. &c., in their said church every year for 90 years. To Philip his son and his assigns for term of his life he bequeaths all that his "Chaumbre and Stuff of Chamberyng thereto bilongyng, which that nowe I occupie and lye ynne my silf, w^t my ij Studies and Countyng houses thereto annexed. Also ij other of my Chambres, whereof oon is w^t a Chapell next adioynyng to my saide Chapell†, on the same side stretching Este and Weste, and abuttith vpon the south toward the grete place late myne, and nowe bilongyng to

---

* (?) Sheriff of London, 16 Hen. VII. 1500.   † (?) Chambre.

Robert Hardyng, goldesmyth, in the pish " of St. Peter le Poer,
&c., with free access to and from the same. The residue of his said
dwelling place from the day of his month's mind to remain to
Elizabeth his wife for term of her life, with remainder after her
decease to his son Philip, &c. To his wife Elizabeth he also
bequeaths for term of her life his "grete place," with tenements
and appurtenances, in the parish of St. Margaret Lothbury, and
also his place called " grene gate," * &c., in the parish of St.
Andrew Cornhill, on the condition that the said Elizabeth, nor any
one on her behalf, do not vex or annoy his executors, &c.,
with reference to the distribution of his property, and after
her decease the same to remain to Philip his son, &c. &c.
To Philip his son he leaves the brewhouse of the Swan, in
the parish of St. Botolph without " Aldrichgate," and to the said
Philip and his heirs, after the death of said Elizabeth, he bequeaths
all his places and tenements, &c., in the parish of St. Andrew
Cornhill and Lime Street, formerly belonging to Philip Malpas,
and to the said Philip he also leaves his brewhouse called the
Garland, &c. in the parish of St. Andrew Eastcheap, and also his
place called the Wharf in the parish of St. Botolph Billingsgate,
also his two shops in the parish of St. Magnus, and his tavern
and brewhouse called the Bear and Dolphin in the parish of St.
Olave and St. Mary Magdalen in Southwark, and also his lands,
&c., in Whitchurch, in the county of Chester, and in the county of
Surrey, with provision for remainder in event of failure of heirs
to Philip, &c. To John Vale his servant he bequeaths an annual
rent of 4*l.* for term of his life, to issue out of his places in the parish
of St. Helen's and " St. Albourgh"† within Bishopsgate Ward, and
further directs that all the said places and the residue of all his tenements called " black Alee," to remain wholly to Philip his son
during the end and term of an indenture made to him for certain
years, &c. under the seal of the Prioress and convent of St. Helen's ;
then follows provision for remainder, and conditions respecting
same if Philip die without heirs. He also bequeaths to John
Forster and Johanne his wife (whom he describes as his daughter)
all those his tenements which sometime belonged to John Maldy,

* Inherited from Philip Malpas.   † St. Ethelburga.

&c. in the parish of St. Olave, against the Bridge House in Southwark, and after the decease of Elizabeth his wife all those his tenements, &c., in the parish of St. Swithin, in London, &c. To Philip his son, and his heirs, he leaves his manor of Gidea or Geddy Hall and Easthouse, &c. with all the ploughs, carts, &c.; and also all his mills, tenements, &c., in the parishes of Hornchurch and Romford, in Essex, also his manor called Bedford's, and his place called "Revles,"* and his place called "Tilehous;" also his manor of Reden Court, and his places and tenements called "Actonys" and "frethes," &c. in the parish of Hornchurch; also his manor of "Haughannes, and his place called "Martynes," in the parishes and towns of "Chigwell, Lambourn, Hetunboise, Stapilforde Abbat, and a brigge,"† in the county of Essex; with provision for remainder in default of issue of said Philip. He also bequeaths unto said Philip his manor called "Maudelen lawser" and his Limekyln, &c., at Stifford Bridge, in the county of Essex. To Aluere Cornebourgh‡ he bequeaths his tenement called "Willotys" (in which Bernarde Tilemaker is described as then dwelling), on condition that he pay his executors 5*l.*, and also discharge his heirs for ever of all quit-rents going out of his manor of Gidea Hall, or otherwise the said tenement to remain to Philip his son.

He also wills that his executors make or cause to be made to the vicar and wardens of the church of St. Nicholas of Witham, in the county of Essex, a lawful estate in fee for evermore of all those his tenements called "ffresles" in the parish of Witham, to yearly keep and hold an obit in said church for his soul, &c. and the souls of Thomas Bassett, John Debenham, John Maldy, and William Thurston, &c. &c. To Philip his son he also bequeaths his place called the Bell and the Angel, in Newland, in Witham, and also his places called Pages and the Mote, &c., in the parish and town of Witham, and also in the towns of "Revnale, Cressyng, Falbo'n, and Brakstede," in the county of Essex, with remainder to William his son, if Philip die without issue; and if

* (?) Nerles.
† Heybridge.
‡ Avery Cornburgh, of Gooshays, in the parish of Romford, died 1486.

William die, then remainder to Thomas Downe (whom he describes as his nephew) and his heirs for evermore. To John his son and his heirs he bequeaths all that his great place called the Swan in Brentwood, in the county of Essex, and all other his tenements, lands, &c., in the town and parish of Brentwood. The said John to have, to him and his heirs, after decease of Elizabeth his wife, all that his manor of Belhouse, and his places called " Morells " and "Boyeles," and his lands called "Tyleherstes," &c., in the county of Essex; and also all his rent of assize and quit rent called Porter's Fee, in the county of Essex, with provision for remainder in event of John dying without heirs. To William his son and his heirs, when he is of lawful age, he bequeaths all his places and tenements in the town of Colchester, in the county of Essex; and also his fishing wears within the Colne Water, between St. Osyth's and Colchester; also all that his beer-house between the "Forthe of Stratford Bow and Stratford Langthorn," in the parish of Witham, in the county of Essex; also all his messuages and tenements in the parish of Eastham. And to the said William and his heirs, after the decease of Elizabeth his wife, he bequeaths his place called "Appultones," &c. in the parish of Chigwell: also all his meadows, &c., in Stratford Langthorn, &c., which late belonged to Philip Malpas, &c. He also wills and ordains that all his ffeoffees enfeoffed to his use of his lands, &c., in the towns of "Erehith, Lesnes, Maideston, Loose fferte, Boughton Monchesey, Redmersh^am, Bapchilde, Milstede," and in the hundred of Middleton, or in other places in the county of Kent, shall make estate thereof to such persons as his executors shall require, and that the said estates be sold, and the proceeds to be applied in payment of his debts, &c. &c.

This will was proved at Lambeth the 1st day of June, 1478.

Although it is not my intention in this paper to enter into the history of the several eminent men of the past and present day who derive their descent from Philip Malpas and Sir Thomas Cooke, still, as the matter will, I have no doubt, be of considerable interest to genealogists, I have added hereto a pedigree of the Cooke family, in addition to the following abstract of the will of Sir Anthony Cooke, the father of the Ladies Burghley, Bacon, and Russell.

Sir Anthony Cooke, great-grandson of Sir Thomas Cooke, as will be seen by the pedigree, died 11th June, and was buried 21st June, 1576, at Romford. By his last will and testament,* dated 22nd May, 1576, he describes himself as' " Anthonye Cooke of Guydyhall in Haveringe, knight." He desires his body to be buried at Romford. To his son Richard, his " daughter Burleighe," his " daughter Bacon," his " daughter Russell," his " daughter Killegrewe," and his son William, he leaves to each a legacy of silver plate. He also bequeaths to his son Richard all his household stuff, &c., at Gidea Hall and Bedfords, &c. Of his books he bequeaths two Latin books and one Greek book to each of his daughters, and the residue to his son Richard and Anthony his son. Also he bequeaths to Richard and William his sons jointly the lease for the term yet to come of his farm at Minster, in the Isle of Thanet, with all stock and cattle. To his son Richard he bequeaths 200*l*. and to his son William 500*l*. He appoints the Right Hon. Sir Nicholas Bacon, knt. Lord Keeper of the Great Seal of England, the Right Hon. the Lord Burghley, Lord Treasurer of England, and his two sons Richard and William Cooke, his executors; and to the Lords Bacon and Burghley he bequeaths 200*l*. each for their pains. All the residue of his goods he bequeaths to Richard Cooke his son.

Then follows his last will and testament of all his lands, &c.

To his son William Cooke and his wife he bequeaths the manor of " Mawdlyn Laver," " Marshallesburie," " Haughaims," and " Wythers," in the county of Essex, with such remainders as was covenanted between himself and Lady Grey upon the marriage of his said son William. To his daughter-in-law, the wife of his son Richard, he bequeaths for the term of her life the manor of Chadwell, &c., and the manor of Reden Court, in Havering, both in the county of Essex, in full recompense of all jointure and dower, &c. To his son Richard and his heirs male he bequeaths all the residue of his lands, with provision for remainder in default of heirs.

* Prerog. Reg. 10 Daughtry.

This will is signed "Anthonie Cooke, 9th June, 1576," from which I infer that it was not signed till some time after it had been drawn up. The witnesses to the signature being W. Burghley; Gabr. Goodman, Dean of Westminster; W. Cooke; George Harrison, notary; Richard Cooke's wife; Henry Killegrewe's wife; and John Escott.

To the will is appended a schedule of legacies, as follows: To Lady Oxford, 50*l*. To Lord Leicester, the choice of two stallions out of Havering Park. *To Robert Cecil*, 20*l*. *To Elizabeth Cecil*, 20*l*. To his daughter Killegrewe, 60*l*. *To Anthony Bacon*, 20*l*. *To Francis Bacon*, 20*l*. To Edward Hoby, 10*l*. To Thomas Posthumus Hoby, 10*l*. To Marie Cooke, three "Portigues." To Anne Cooke, three "Portigues."* To Anne Killegrewe five "Portigues." To his cousin Skinner 10*l*. and to his cousin Ogle 5*l*. To John Escott his servant, 3*l*. 5*s*. 8*d*. To Edward Davie his servant, 3*l*. To Richard Howell his servant, 3*l*. To every of the three servingmen in his household at the time of his death, 40*s*. each. To every other "hinde," woman servant, and boy, being to the number of fifteen in his household at the time of his decease, 20*s*. each, &c.

This will was proved at London, 5th March, 1576.

It will be seen that I have adopted throughout the spelling of the surname of Cooke as it occurs in the wills of Sir Thomas and his great-grandson Sir Anthony Cooke, although the name often appears as Coke in the various records and chronicles.

In concluding this paper, I have to express my thanks to E. J. Sage, Esq. for the kind loan of his MS. pedigree and notes of the Cooke family, and also to my friend Thomas Milbourn, Esq. for other information relating to the family.

* A gold coin of the value of 3*l*. 10*s*.

FAMILY, OF GIDEA HALL, ROMFORD, CO. ESSEX.

COOKE.

SIR THOMAS COOKE, Knight, Romford, draper; Sheriff 14 1462; died 1478; bur. in A

1. Sir Philip Cooke, Knight, of Gidea Hall; born 1454; living 1478. Dubbed a Bridge Foot, at the King's entry into London after the Battle of Blackheath 1

John Cooke, Esquire, of Gidea Hall; died=Alice (Elizabe 1510; buried in the church of the Crutched | Sanders, Esqu Friars, near the Tower of London. | and Oxfordshi

SIR ANTHONY COOKE, Knight, of Gidea Hall; born 1504; High Preceptor to Edward VI.; died 11 and buried 2

| Richard Cooke, Esquire, of Gidea Hall=Anne, dau. of John Cawn- | 2. William Cooke, Esquire, second son,=Frances, dau. of Lord John Grey, of High Steward of the Liberty of Havering | ton, Esquire, of London; | of St. Martin's in the Fields, London; | Pirgo in Havering, co. Essex, (brother atte Bower; died 3 and buried 12 of Oct. | buried at Romford 25 Sept. | born at Romford; died 14, bur. 19 May, | to the Duke of Suffolk); mar. at Rom- 1579, at Romford, aged 48. | 1617. | 1589, in St. Martin's Church. | ford 26 Aug. 1569; bur. at St.Martin's, 30 Jan. 1606.

Sir Anthony Cooke, Knight, of Gidea=Avise, dau. of Sir William | Philippa, wife to | 1. William Cooke, | 2. Sir William Cooke, Knight,= Hall, High Steward of the Liberty of | Waldegrave, of Smallbridge, | Hercules Meautys, | bapt. at St. Mar- | of Highnam, co. Gloucester; Havering; born about 1559; knighted | co. Suffolk; bur. at St. Martin's | Esquire, of West- | tin's, 21 Sept. 1574, | bapt. 14 Feb. 1578-9, at Rom- by the Earl of Essex in 1596; buried at | in the Fields, 5 Oct. 1642. | ham, co. Essex. | and buried there 5 | ford; bur. at St. Martin's, 4 Romford 28 Dec. 1604. | | | July, 1579. | March, 1619.

FOR ISSUE SEE B.   FOR ISSUE

1. Sir Edward Cooke, Knight, of Gidea Hall; High Steward=Martha, dau. of Sir William Daniell, Knight, Chief Justice | 2. Sir Hercules Francis Co of Havering atte Bower; bapt. at Romford 3 March, 1579-80; | of the Common Pleas; mar. at Hornchurch 25 Sept. 1606; | Liberty of Havering atte I buried there 20 July, 1626. | buried at Romford 27 April, 1643. | county, 1634; died before

| Charles Cooke, of Gidea Hall, ob. s.p.; | Edward Cooke, bur. | Elizabeth, buried at | Anne, dau. and coheir, bapt. 25 Sept. 1610, at Romfo buried at Romford 7 Aug. 1629. | at Romford 1 Dec. | Romford 13 March, | Hall, by whom she had issue five sons and five daugh | 1609. | 1616. | Lady Sydenham was buried at Romford 9 August, 16

James Cecil, third Earl, K.G.=Margaret, third daughter o Earl of Rt

James Cecil, fourth Earl, K.G.=Frances, dau. and coheir of Sheriff 1684 and Lo

James Cecil, fifth Earl.=Anne, second dau. and coh Tufton, sixth Earl

James Cecil, sixth Earl.=Elizabeth, eldest dau. of Ed and sister to the Rev.

James Cecil, seventh Earl and first=Mary Amelia, second dau. Marquess of Salisbury, K.G. | 1597, Lord Mayor of Londo Sheriff 1569, Lord Mayor o

Frances Mary, first wife, dau. and sole heir of Bamber Gascoyne, Esquire, (and great-grand-daughter to=James Brownlow William G Sir Crisp Gascoyne, brewer, Alderman of Vintry Ward, Sheriff 1747, Lord Mayor of London 1752). | and second Marques

ROBERT ARTHUR TALBOT GASCOYNE CECIL, second son, third and present Marquess of=Georgiana, eldest daughter Salisbury, late Secretary of State for India, P.C. M.P. | Har

COMPILED from the Gene

COOKE FAMILY, OF GIDEA HALL, ROMFORD, CO. ESSEX.

A.*

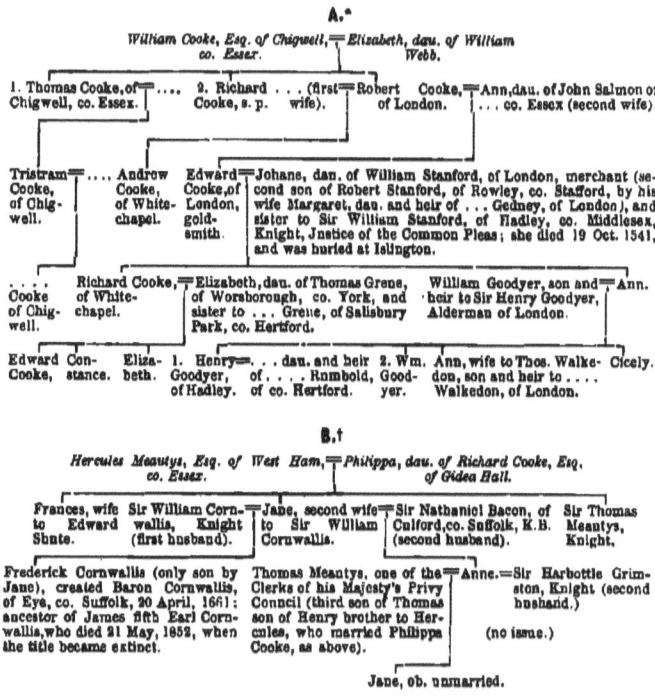

William Cooke, Esq. of Chigwell,⹀Elizabeth, dau. of William
co. Essex. Webb.

1. Thomas Cooke, of⹀... 2. Richard ... (first⹀Robert Cooke,⹀Ann, dau. of John Salmon of
Chigwell, co. Essex. Cooke, s. p. wife). of London. co. Essex (second wife).

Tristram⹀... Andrew Edward⹀Johans, dau. of William Stanford, of London, merchant (se-
Cooke, Cooke, Cooke, of cond son of Robert Stanford, of Rowley, co. Stafford, by his
of Chig- of White- London, wife Margaret, dau. and heir of ... Gedney, of London), and
well. chapel. gold- sister to Sir William Stanford, of Hadley, co. Middlesex,
smith. Knight, Justice of the Common Pleas; she died 19 Oct. 1541,
and was buried at Islington.

.... Richard Cooke,⹀Elizabeth, dau. of Thomas Grene, William Goodyer, son and⹀Ann.
Cooke of White- of Worsborough, co. York, and heir to Sir Henry Goodyer,
of Chig- chapel. sister to ... Grene, of Salisbury Alderman of London.
well. Park, co. Hertford.

Edward Con- Eliza- 1. Henry⹀... dau. and heir 2. Wm. Ann, wife to Thos. Walke- Cicely.
Cooke, stance. beth. Goodyer, of ... Rumbold, Good- don, son and heir to ....
of Hadley. of co. Hertford. yer. Walkedon, of London.

B.†

Hercules Meautys, Esq. of West Ham,⹀Philippa, dau. of Richard Cooke, Esq.
co. Essex. of Gidea Hall.

Frances, wife Sir William Corn-⹀Jane, second wife⹀Sir Nathaniel Bacon, of Sir Thomas
to Edward wallis, Knight to Sir William Culford, co. Suffolk, K.B. Meautys,
Shute. (first husband). Cornwallis. (second husband). Knight.

Frederick Cornwallis (only son by Thomas Meautys, one of the⹀Anne.=Sir Harbottle Grim-
Jane), created Baron Cornwallis, Clerks of his Majesty's Privy ston, Knight (second
of Eye, co. Suffolk, 20 April, 1661 ; Council (third son of Thomas husband.)
ancestor of James fifth Earl Corn- son of Henry brother to Her-
wallis, who died 21 May, 1852, when cules, who married Philippa (no issue.)
the title became extinct. Cooke, as above).

Jane, ob. unmarried.

C.‡

Sir William Cooke, Knight, of Highnam,⹀Lucy, dau. of Sir Thomas Lucy, Knight,
co. Gloucester. of Charlecote, co. Warwick.

1. Sir Ro-=Dorothy, dau. 2. William 3. Thomas Elizabeth Frances. Doro- Mil- Anne.
bert of Sir Miles Cooke. Cooke. wife of John thy. dred.
Cooke, Fleetwood, of Scudamore.
of High- Aldwincle, of Kent-
nam, co. Northamp- church, co.
Knight. ton, Receiver Warwick.
of the Court
of Wards.

Authorities for the above Pedigrees.

* Harl. MS. Brit. Mus. No. 1541, ff. 42 b-43 ; No. 1077, f. 53 ; and No. 1439, f. 84, &c.
† Clutterbuck's *Hist. of Herts*, vol. 1. p. 93, and Burke's *Extinct and Dormant Peerages.*
‡ Harl. MS. Brit. Mus. No. 1543, f. 48 b.

JOHN CADE'S FOLLOWERS IN KENT.

PREPARED FOR
THE MEETING OF THE KENT ARCHÆOLOGICAL SOCIETY AT ASHFORD,
BY
WILLIAM DURRANT COOPER, F.S.A., V.P. OF THE SUSSEX AND MIDDLESEX ARCHÆOLOGICAL SOCIETIES, ETC. ETC.

A MEETING of the Kent Archæological Society at Ashford would have been incomplete, if there had been no notice taken of the great rising in 1450 of the "Commons of Kent," under Cade, their "captain," who has been called (though erroneously) "the Tanner of Ashford."

Ashford and its neighbourhood was undoubtedly the heart of the rising, and it was generally supported throughout the lathe of Scray, as it was also in the lathes of Aylesford and Sutton at Hone. There were comparatively few places in the lathe of Shepway, from whence adherents were drawn to the cause; and, with the exception of the hundreds of Eastry, Petham, Preston, Wingham, and the Isle of Thanet, the lathe of St. Augustine was free from the rising.

The particulars relating to this rising,—the dates of the chief events, the station of the persons engaged, the extent of the districts in Kent, Sussex, Surrey, and Essex, from which contingents came, and the time of the pardons under which the great body dispersed,—have all been involved in doubt and obscurity. Yet the Patent Roll of 28th Hen. VI. (part 2, m. 13, etc.), contains the materials for supplying many of these wanting particulars. It has upon it the names of many hundreds of forces of the therein acknowledged "John Mortimer's" followers, who were pardoned, and in many cases their designations and trades.

It has been admitted, indeed, that Cade drew to himself some "tall men" of this county; yet it is not known how many were of old and good families, many remaining to this day. It is worth while at the outset to give their names.

JOHN CADE'S FOLLOWERS IN KENT. 25

There was 1 Knight—
*Cheyne, John, of East Church, in the Isle of Sheppey.
18 Esquires also appear, viz.:—
Hexstall, William, of East Peckham.[1]
Ysaake, John, of Patrykesbourne.[2]
Pympe, Thomas, of All Saints, in the Hundred of Hoo.
Appuldurfeld, Thos., } of Faversham.
Thornbury, John,[3] }
Mareys, William, of Preston, near Faversham.
Edward, William, of Sandhurst.[4]
*Fyneux, John.[5]
Drury, John, of Sandwich.
Ildergate, John, of Sandwich.
Ballard, Thomas, of East Greenwich.
*Culpeper, William, of Goudhurst.
Haute, William.
Burgeys, Thomas, of Gravene.
Seyncler, John, of Faversham.
*Fogge, John, of Chart.
Clyfford, John, of Bobbing.
*Norton, William, of Sheldwych.[6]

The names only of the five families marked with an asterisk are to be found in the "Visitation of the County," in 1579.

74 Gentlemen[7] are also named, viz.:—
Appelton, Henry, of Buckwell, in Boughton Aluph.
Miller, John, of Holingbourne.
Spert, William, of Halden.
Hogge, Stephen, of Frittenden.
*Norton, Stephen, of Chart next Sutton.

[1] The heiress of this family married William Whetenhall.
[2] Sheriff, 1461. The heiress of this family married a Sydley, and then Sir Henry Palmer.
[3] He had been sheriff in 1446.
[4] In another pardon, as gentleman.
[5] This was probably an uncle of the future Chief Justice of the King's Bench.
[6] In another pardon as gentleman.
[7] A list of the Gentlemen of Kent in 12 Hen. VI. is given by Fuller, and reprinted by Harris, p. 441; several of these names appear there.

E

Goolde, John,
Grovehurst, Richard, } of Middleton.
Buntyng, John,
Bernes, Robert,
(in two pardons,) } of Hawkhurst.
*Congeherst, John,[1]
*Roberd, John, Senior and Jr., of Cranbrook.
Cattys, John, of Wrotham.
(In two pardons.)
Penwortham, John, and
Belde, William } of Canterbury.
(in two pardons),
Edward, William, of Sandhurst.
Hethe, Thomas, of Woolwich.
Lovelace, Richard, of Byngesdom.
———— William, of Bethersden.
Northampton, William, of Woolwich.
Ball, Robert, of Thornham.
*Martyn, John,
Aleyn, Robert, } of Dartford.
Appleton, Roger, Senr. and Junr.,
Rowe, John, of Bexley.
—— Robert,
—— William, } of Aylesford.
Somery, Robert, of Staplehurst.
Elys, John, of Otham.
*Twysden, Roger,[2]
*Gybbes, John, } of Great Chart.
Bird, John, of Clynton.
Hope, James,
Oxenden, John, } of Wingham.
*Renne, Thomas, of Renham.
Clyfton, Robert, of Clyfton.
*Norton, William, of Sheldwych.
Forde, Richard, of Penshurst.

[1] Mildred, the heiress of the family, married John Scott, and carried the estate to him.
[2] He married Jane, daughter of —— Cooper, of Stone.

Chamberleyn, John, otherwise } of East Farleigh.
Smethcote, John,
Langley, Walter, of Estry.
Wynterborne, William, of Esshetefford or Wy.
Stone, John, Jr.
Vaghen, John, of Gravesend.
Chertesey, Edmund, of Rochester.
      Same,   of Headcorn.
*Culpeper, Richard, of East Farleigh.
Cardon, Thomas, and } of Clyve.
,,   John,
Est, Robert, } of Maidstone.
Dyne, Richard,
Tragosse, Thomas, of Boughley.
Odyerne, William, of Wittersham.
Ridley, Roger, of Canterbury.
Culpepyr, John, } of Goudhurst.
*   ,,   Richard,
*Gylford, John, of Dolling.[1]
Walleys, William, of Dover.
Chymbham, Edmund, of Southfleet.
Chertesey, Edmund, of Headcorn.
*Bettenham, Robert, of Pluckley.
*Brokman, William, and
    ,,   John, } of Assheteford.
Godewyn, Hugh,
Barbour, William, of Feversham.
Payne, John, } of Mereworth.
Chamberleyn, Robert,
*Cheynewe, James, of Westerham.
Downe, John, and } of Westmalling.
Langley, Robert,
Atte Wood, Hugh, of Yalding.
Kelsham, Thomas.
Brencheley, Walter, of Denynden.

[1] He married daughter and heir of ———— Worsley, of Sloworthe, and their heiress Margaret married William Cotton.

The names of the yeomen are very numerous, and several of them have risen to the rank of gentry, such as the Courthopes, Tonges, Springetts, and Woodgates : whilst some of the old names, such as the Septvans, now lost, were then to be found.

It was not a disorganised mob, nor a chance gathering. In several Hundreds the constables duly, and as if legally, summoned the men; and many parishes, particularly Marden, Penshurst,[1] Hawkhurst, Northfleet, Boughton-Malherbe, Smarden, and Pluckley, furnished as many men as could be found, in our own day, fit for arms. Among those pardoned are the towns of Canterbury, Chatham, Maidstone, Rochester, and Sandwich; John Browne, the Bailiff of Folkestone, and John Cockeram, the Mayor of the new town of Queenborough; the constables of the Hundreds of Eastry, Petham, Preston, Ringslowe,[2] and Wingham, in the lathe of St. Augustine; of Chatham, Gillingham, Hoo, Littlefield, Maidstone, Shamwell, Thwyford, and Wrotham, in the lathe of Aylesford; of Boughton-under-Chart, Longbridge, Felborough, Milton, and Teynham, in the lathe of Scray; of Langport, in the lathe of Shepway; of Dartford, Blackheath, Bromley, Beckenham, Codsheath, Lessness, Ruxley, and Somerden, in the lathe of Sutton at Hone.

In East Greenwich and Dartford, which were close to the Camp at Blackheath, the wives of many men were included in the pardons, having doubtless entertained the men assembled in arms.

In Sussex the Abbot of Battle and the Prior of Lewes participated in the rising;[3] but in Kent the only names of ecclesiastics which appear are five, viz.:

Clerke, John, Parson of the church of Halgeste, in the Hundred of Hoo, in three pardons.

Changle, Thomas, of Yalding.

Spencer, Henry, Chaplain of Cowling.

Botcler, John, of Boughton Malherbe.

Penyngton, William, Chaplain of Osprynge.

---

[1] Penshurst, at this time, belonged to the exiled Duke of Buckingham.
[2] One is John Septvans.
[3] See *post*, where the pardons for Sussex are given.

And two "Holy-water clerkes," being the persons who carried the holy water.

Among the occupations are some which mark the transition of the English language; thus Butchers, in most parishes, are in others called Fleshers; Cordwainer and Corvesor are used indiscriminately; Sonderer, otherwise Baker or New Baker; Ripiers, who carried the fish to London; Ferrour for farrier, and Putter for the carriers of wood to make charcoal. One notary and one scrivener, are here; one goldsmith, from Maidstone, and one trumpeter, from Holingbourne. The fullers and tanners are also here, and chapmen, haberdashers, drapers, mercers, tailors, and glovers; chandlers, and wax- and tallow-chandlers; grocers, spicers, and bakers; braziers, tinkers, sawyers, carpenters, masons, tilers, thatchers, turners, smiths, coopers, and saddlers; of barbers, more than a dozen; and brewers, innholders, vintners, and taverners; a solitary hackney-man, two grooms, and a servant. As might be anticipated in a maritime county, there are shipmen, watermen, and mariners. The manufactures are represented by clothmakers and webbes, or weavers in Smarden and Pluckley. In many parishes the occupations are not given; but the main force consisted of husbandmen and labourers.

It is incorrectly stated by Holinshed that the men abruptly withdrew themselves and deserted Cade so soon as they were shown pardons by the Chancellor (Kempe) and the Bishop of Winchester (Waynfleete). The Chronicle of William of Wyrcester (p. 76 *et seq.*) gives the correct detail of the negotiation with Cade in the church of St. Margaret Southwark, on the 6th July (the morning after the indecisive fight on London Bridge). Cade is designated John Mortimer in his pardon, which is dated on (Monday) the very day of the negotiations, as appears by the Patent Roll. On the same day are dated the pardons for John Robynson, William Bygge, Simon Morley, and John Swayn, of the city of Canterbury; but the remainder of the pardons bear date the following day (Tuesday), 7th July.

The number of names entered on the Patent Roll shows that accurate muster-rolls must have been kept; and the appearance of the same parish in different parts of the roll may indicate that the persons took part in the two different parts of the rising, for two parts there were.

Kent had been discontented in the early part of the year 1450. Thomas Cheyney, a fuller, of Canterbury, "calling himself an heremite cleped *Blew-berd*," had been taken on 9th February, at Canterbury, for raising a rebellion.[1] He was executed, and his head ordered to be sent to that city; but so great was his popularity, that the sheriffs of London had much difficulty in conveying it, "as unneth any persones durst nor wolde take upon hem the caridge,"[2] for doubt of their lives.

The Duke of Suffolk was taken off Dover on 2nd May, and killed. Lord Say, who lived at Knole, was Lord-Lieutenant; his son-in-law, William Crowmer, was Sheriff, and the threats they held out against the "Commons of Kent" brought matters to a crisis.

I give the several dates from the Chronicle of William of Wyrcester.

Whitsunday was on 24th May, and in that week the insurrection of the commons of Kent alone began. On 1st June, the camp was fixed at Blackheath; on Sunday, 7th, the King came to London, and on 11th set out against the rebels. But they had decamped in the night, and retired to Sevenoaks. They were followed by two Staffords, who, with twenty-four followers, were killed at Sevenoaks. The King then went to Kenilworth. At the end of the month, Cade and his followers were joined by strong contingents from Sussex and Surrey. They made a second march to Blackheath. On Friday, 3rd July, they entered London city, and were met by a good number from Essex. On 4th, James Fynes, Lord Say, was beheaded at the Standard in Chepe and his son-in-law, Crowmer, without Aldgate. The citizens were pillaged, and on the night of Sunday, 5th July, they rose and fought Cade and his men on London Bridge.

On the morning of the 6th began the negociations with Cade for "a charter of pardon from the King *for them all;*" but as a preliminary, Cade insisted and obtained the acceptance by the

[1] Stowe's Annals, p. 388.   [2] Ellis' Letters, ser. 2, vol. i. p. 115.

Chancellor and Bishop Waynfleet of the Bill of Petitions, which had been refused by the Privy Council. The complaints of the commons of Kent comprised fifteen heads; they are printed at length in Stowe's Annals, p. 388, and the following are the particular grievances of the county:—

" 1. It is openly noysed that Kent should be destroyed with royall power, and made a wild forest, for the death of the Earl of Suffolke, of which the commons were never guilty."

And, after complaining that the King lived on his commons, whilst his own revenues were held by other men; that the lords of the royal blood had been put out of his presence,[1] and other mean persons of lower nature exalted to be of his Privy Council; that the stuff and purveyance for the King's household had not been paid for; that people were impeached and indicted to have grants obtained of their land; that divers poor people and commons of the realm, having perfect title to their land, had that title impeached and could not pursue their right; that the King's lands in France had been alienated; and requiring that the traitors who did it should be punished; they say:—

" 8. Collectors of the 15 peny in Kent be greatly vexed and hurt in paying great sums of money in the Exchequer to sue out a writ called *Quorum nomina*, for allowance of the Barons of the Ports, which now is desired that hereafter in the lieu of the collectors the Barons aforesaid may sue it out for their ease at their own costs."[2]

And then, having complained of the excessive surety or bail taken by the sheriffs; and of feigned indictments against simple and poor people that use not hunting; and of the returns of amerciaments called "the Green Waxe," without summons or warning; they proceed:—

[1] In his own requests Cade expressly names the exiled Duke of York.

[2] This was a writ to prove the exemption of the Barons of the Cinque Ports resident within the county parishes from liability to contribute to the subsidies.

"12. The ministers of the Court of Dover, in Kent, vex and arrest divers people through all the shire, out of castle-ward, passing bands (bounds) and liberty used of old time, by divers subtle and untrue means and actions falsely feined, taking great fee at their lust, in great hurt of the people in all their shire of Kent.

"13. The people of the said shire of Kent may not have their free election in the choosing of knights of the shire, but letters have been sent from divers estates to the great rulers of all the country, the which enforceth their tenants and other people by force to choose other persons than the common will is.[1]

"14. Whereas knights of the shire should choose the King's collectors indifferently, without any bribe-taking; they have sent now late to divers persons, notifying to them to be collectors, whereupon gifts and bribes be taken, and so the collector's office is bought and sold extortionously at the knights' lust.[2]

"15. The people be sore vexed in costs and labour, called to the sessions of peace in the said shire, appearing from the furthest and uttermost parts of the west into the east, the which causeth to some men five days' journey; whereupon they desire the said appearance to be divided into two parts,[3] the which one part to appear in one place, another part in another place; in relieving of the grievance and intolerable labours and vexations of the said people."

Cade also charged Stephen Slegg, who was the sheriff in the previous year (1449), William Isle, who twice represented the county, and Robert Est, as being extortioners.

This is not the place to comment on the political importance of

---

[1] The right of election for counties, which, like the election of coroners, had been in *all* the freeholders, had been limited, by an Act of this reign, 8 Hen. VI. c. 7 (1430), to freeholders who could expend 40s., equivalent to £20 now.

[2] James Fynes and William Crowmer had been members, the latter in two parliaments.

[3] A like complaint of the inconvenience of the Sussex County Courts was remedied by Act 19 Hen. VII. c. 24, and they were to be held in West Sussex and East Sussex alternately.

the demands made, nor can we now judge of the accuracy of the complaints; all that I need remark is the wide difference between them and the travestie of them given by Shakspeare.

On receiving pardons, the main body of the commons dispersed, but Cade alleged that the pardons were insufficient without the sanction of Parliament (they are undoubtedly tested at Westminster, where the King was not), and persuaded a remnant of his followers to remain in arms. He retired with them to Rochester, having previously sent there the plate, jewels, and money which had been taken during the rising. They failed in an attack upon Queenborough castle, which was successfully defended by Sir Roger Chamberleyn[1] and two men. Geoffry Kechyn and another, called "Capitaignes Boucher," were taken; and a third, William Parmenter, also calling himself "a captain of Kent," with other principals, were placed in the custody of Thomas Waryn, and then sent to the castles of Windsor and Winchester.[2]

In the Act of attainder[3] passed in the Parliament held at Westminster, on the 9th November following, Cade is described as having levied war subsequently to his pardon,[4] viz., at Southwark, on the 8th July, at Deptford and Rochester, on the 9th, and also at Rochester and elsewhere, on the 10th and 11th July. The King's proclamation was issued on the 10th July; the assumed name of Mortimer used in the pardon of the 6th was dropped; he was called John Cade, and a reward of 1000 marks[5] was offered for him; and a further reward of 5 marks for any of those who should from that day forth accompany him. In fact, "disguised in a strange attire, he privily fled into the wood country, beside Lewes in Sussex, hoping to escape."

He was pursued by Alexander Iden, the new sheriff of Kent, and by "others with him," and not alone. On what day they came up with Cade at Heathfield, is not clear; in the Chronicle

---

[1] As a reward he received a payment in the following year. See Devon's Issue Roll, p. 471.   [2] Ibid. 472.
[3] The remainder of this portion down to the names at p. 40 was printed in vol. 18 of the Sussex Archæological Collections.
[4] 29 Hen. VI. c. 1.   [5] Not crowns as Shakespeare has it.

published by the Camden Society,[1] in 1850, it is stated that he was wounded " unto the dethe, and take and carried in a cart toward Londoun, and be the way deide." By the 15th July, 1450, Iden and his aiders had brought the dead body to the council; on that day the King ordered the Treasurer and Chamberlains of his Exchequer,[2] out of the goods, jewells, and chattels which had come to their hands, and over which Cade's servants had quarrelled, to deliver the 1,000 marks in money to the use of Iden, and of "the said persones that brought the body."[3] The King gave £20, of his own special grace, to John Davy, for the good services rendered by him in taking "that great traitor and rebel, who called himself John Mortymer, at Hefeld," in Sussex. His head was stuck on London Bridge, with the face towards Kent, and his body quartered. One quarter was sent to Blackheath; a second to Norwich, where the Bishop (Walter Harp) was supposed to favour the cause of the Duke of York; a third to Salisbury; and the fourth to Gloucester, the Abbot of St. Peter's there being also a favourer of the cause.[4] Two followers of Cade were also beheaded: the quarters of one, Nicholas Jakes, were sent to Chichester, Rochester, Portsmouth, and Colchester; and those of John Rammesey, wine drawer, to Stamford, Coventry, Newbury, and Winchester,[5] showing how widely spread were the opinions of the " commons of Kent."

Iden is called " our trusty and well beloved Alexandre Iden, *Shirrief* of our countie of Kent," and he also had 20 marks reward, for taking and conducting to the King Robert Spence, " a sworn brother to the great traitor and rebel calling himself John Mortymer."

The order of 15th July further charged the Treasurer and Chamberlains, if there were any person or persons from whom any of the said " goodes, catelles, and juelx as above, by wey of spoiling or robbing, were taken from," and coming to them,

---

[1] Page 68.

[2] Rymer, Fœdera, tom. xi. p. 275.

[3] Iden was also rewarded by being made keeper of Rochester Castle, with a salary of 36*l.* a-year, out of which he was to pay 16*l.* for repairs. *Rot. Parl.* v. p. 313. See also Devon's Issue Roll, p. 468-9.

[4] Ellis' Letters, ser. 2, vol. i. p. 113.   [5] Ibid. 115.

"for to suee to have them agen," that to him or them as so would sue, "making faith that it was so take" from them, that they should make him be preferred in the buying thereof before any other person, and that they should sell it to him for "lesse or more ease then" it be worth, after their discretion.

The King was no loser by the reward, for there were £105 15s. in cash, and goods were sold on the 29th of the same month (August), for £274 8s. 4d. What those goods jewels, &c. were, we know from the record [1] preserved among the memoranda of the Treasury of the Exchequer. [2]

Imprimis, in money counted CVli. XVs.

Item, in a round boxe of lether, VI parysh cuppes of sylver —IX spones of sylver—I purse wrought in the stole (band to hold it) with XVII counters of sylver—I stone of birell (of green colour for the eye, said Sir Francis Palgrave)—I gerdil of purple not harneysid—a bitores clee [3] harneysed—I muske

---

[1] By Letters Patent, dated 12th July, 1450, Sir Thomas Tirrel, Knight, and Richard Waller, Esq. with others were appointed to arrest and take for the King, and in his name, the goods, chattels, jewels, and sums of money, "which a certain person calling himself John Mortymer, by himself and his adherents in the county of Kent, took and carried away with him," and to put the same under safe custody for the King's behoof, and to carry and transfer them whither it should seem best to them, and to pay such and so many sums thereof to such persons as to them should seem meet for the benefit of the King and his kingdom, especially about the taking of the aforesaid John Mortymer and his adherents." Nevertheless by his writ, dated 18th July, the King commanded the commissioners as soon as they were able to deliver all "such goods and chattels, jewels, and sums of money" to his Treasurer of England and Chamberlains of the Exchequer. Accordingly an Indenture was made 21st July, between the latter of the one part, and Sir Thomas Tirrell and Richard Waller, Esq. of the other part, and by virtue of the writ they delivered at the receipt of the Exchequer the "certain goods, jewels, and sums of money," set out above.

[2] Calendars and Inventories, vol. ii. p. 217.

[3] Mr. John Gongh Nichols has kindly suggested that the writer may have intended "Bicores," and the article may have been something pretended to have been the claw of the fabulous animal, the hicorn. In Dodsley's Collection of Old Plays, is a short poem by Lydgate, on Bycorne and Chichevache. See a letter by T. Wright, in the Gent. Mag. for July, 1834, p. 43. In old inventories unicorns' horns, or articles made of them, often occur, and various pretended parts of fabulous animals." A drawing is in Lemon's Calendar of Soc. of Ant. Papers, &c.

balle (to smell at)—I stone of berall harneysid—II laces of sylke.

Item, in two trussyng cofers (baskets used for carrying large parcels of goods) and in two gardevyances (chests or trunks)—I salt saler of silvere and gilt castell wyse with III small salt salers in III corners and the IIII lakkith—I chalyce of golde garnyshed with peerls and I paten thereto—II chargeours and XIJ litell disshes of silvere—II bolles of silver—I nutte coveryd—III chaced cuppes—I covercle of a salt saler—VIII sponys of silver—III knoppes of cuppes—a coler of sylver—I paire of knyves—II purses—a diall of silver—III salers (salt cellars), of silver with a covercle of a cuppe—I chalys of gold with a paten—I horn harneysed with silver and gilt—I saler of gold coveryd, garnyshed with saphires and perlys—I ewer of silver—II potell pottes (two quarts) gilt—I spyce plate of silver and gilt—II stondyng cuppes of one sute coveryd, swaged, and pounced (twisted and pierced)—I standing bolle pote coveryd gilt without—I peyre tabell knyves—III in a shethe with gilt haftes—I ewer of silver withoute knoppe—I pece I crewet—I paxbrede (tablet with a representation of the crucifixion) of silver and gilt—I nose of an kandelstyk of silver—I girdill of the old faccyon harneysid with silver—I scalop of sylver I litell piece of reed tarteron (cloth used for curtains)—I pawkener (pouche or pocket) wrought in the stole (band over the shoulder)—I potte of silver of a galon withoute a lidde—I potte contenyng a potell (two quarts) gilt—I quarte potte of silver—I gobelete of the olde faccion—I ymage of silver and gilt—I cuppe coveryd stondyng gilt withoute pomell (ball or knob)—I flatte cuppe coveryd gilt—I salt saler coveryd of sylver—I litell gobelet of sylver coveryd—I chafure (saucepan) of silver—I blak remenaunt of velewet fugury—I olde vestement—I primer with clapses of silver—I peire of shetys—V small pecys of vre (vaire or ermine)—IX peces and remenauntes of baudekyn cloth (silk interwoven with threads of gold)—I stondyng cuppe coveryd and gilt—I flatte cuppe of silver coveryd.

Which same jewels and parcels by virtue of the writ of the Lord the King under his great seal to the Treasurer and

Chamberlains of the Exchequer directed remaining among the mandates of Easter term, in the twenty-eighth year of the said lord the King, were sold by Thomas Rothewell, Clerk of the Treasurer of England, in the stead and names of the said Treasurer and Chamberlains, to divers persons for the sum . . . of which it is answered to the King in the Pells of Receipt for Easter term, in the same 28th year, viz., on the 29th day of August, as more fully there appears in form following, viz.: From Philip Malpas,[1] for goods of the said John Cade, cxiiij. li. ix. s. iiij. d. From Richard Joynour, for goods of the said John Cade, xx. li. From Thomas Rothewell, for goods of the said John Cade, cxxxj. li. ix. s. iij. d. From Thomas Stokdale, for goods of the said John Cade, viij. li. ix. s. x. d.

And it remained in a certain wooden box, in a green chest, under this sign—

"Cade, otherwise called Mortimer."

The acts of the council (vi. 96, 99, 101), July 12 to August 25, contain several orders relative to Cade, and the property seized by him, and an order to deliver to Master Andrew Holes, keeper of the Privy Seal, who was about to undertake a journey for the King, and was destitute of horses, six horses lately belonging to that "traitour calling himself Captain of Kent," by way of loan; and 40*l*. of the goods were given to the bailiffs and citizens of Rochester, to make the East Gate of that city towards Canterbury.

Further steps were taken to bring to punishment such of Cade's adherents as had continued in arms in Kent subsequently to the pardon. Accordingly, on the 1st August, a commission was issued [2] into Kent, to inquire into divers offences committed by persons who had disturbed the public peace within the county of Kent and that county only, no reference being made to the proceedings in Southwark or London; it was in truth a special commission to try those, who, after the pardons, had refused to

---

[1] Was he obliged to buy back his own property? In Devon's Issue Roll, p. 467, it is stated that 114*l*. worth of the jewels stolen out of the house of Malpas belonged to the Duke of York, and that sum was repaid.

[2] Pat. 28 Hen. VI. part 2, m. 17.

return to their homes, and had remained in arms with Cade at Deptford and Rochester; and the proceedings are not open to the censure which Mackintosh [1] implies of being in breach of good faith, and for acts pardoned by the general amnesty.

The commissioners were John (Kempe) Cardinal Archbishop of York (and Chancellor), John (Stafford) Archbishop of Canterbury, William (Waynflete) Bishop of Winchester, Humphrey Duke of Buckingham, Ralph Boteler of Sudeley knt., John Prisote (Chief Justice of Common Pleas), Peter Arderne (Chief Baron of the Exchequer), Thomas Fulthorpe, knt. (J.C. Pleas), William Yelverton (J. K. Bench), Richard Bingham (J.K.B.), Nicholas Asshton (J.C.P.), John Portington (J.C.P.), Robert Danvers (immediately afterwards J.C.P., who had sat as Cade's Justiciary at Guildhall), Wm. Wangford (afterwards Sergeant at Law), Thomas Burgoyne, and Wm. Laken (afterwards J.K.B). It is open to remark and comment that the sound lawyer, then Chief Justice of England (John Fortescue), was not named in the commission; and that the senior judge (Prisote) has been unfavourably remembered for his partiality.[2]

The result of this commission, which was opened at Canterbury, was, " that eight men were judged and executed" there, " and in other towns of Kent and Sussex was done the like execution." [3] A search, however, through the Comptrolment rolls of this period to find the names of the persons tried or executed has not been attended with success.[4]

In the Act of Parliament Cade is called "that false traitor John Cade, naming himself John Mortimer, late Captain of Kent;" and it is said that " tho' dead and mischieved, yet by the law of the land not punished," the King, " to put such traitors in fear in time coming," and by request of the Commons, and by authority of Parliament, ordered that he should be attainted, and should forfeit to the King his "goods, lands, and tenements, rents,

[1] Vol. ii. p. 14.
[2] Foss's Judges, vol. iv. p. 356.
[3] Holinshed.
[4] The names of those tried at Rochester in the subsequent rising are printed in Sir Henry Ellis's Original Letters, 2 ser. vol. 1.

and possessions, which he held on the 8th July or after," and his blood was declared corrupt.

If Cade had been the low-born person he has been represented, no act of attainder would have been of any operation against his lands and tenements, nor would it have been of importance to declare his blood corrupt. He was supposed to be put forward by the Duke of York in order to ascertain the feeling of the nation towards his claims, and hence the assumed name of the Duke's cousin, Mortimer. The name of Cade, however, was not of unfrequent occurrence in the neighbourhood of Heathfield. It is to be found in the subsidy rolls of Mayfield down to 1557. In the subsidy of 1328 we have John and William Le Cade, Robert and Matthew Cade; in 1332 Richard Le Cade, and two Johns, Robert, William, and Matthew Cade; in 1523 we find Ellen Cade, wid.; in 1545 John Cade; in 1558-9 John Cade, with lands worth 4l. a-year; and in 1557, John Cade, with lands worth 40s.[1]

That the consequence of his acts, even after his death, continued to be thought of moment by the Council is evidenced by the fact that the act of 1450 was not deemed sufficient, and in the parliament holden at Reading, two years afterwards (1452),[2] a further act of attainder was passed in which Cade is called the "most abominable tyrant, horrible, odious, and errant false traitor, John Cade, calling and naming himself sometime Mortimer, and sometime Captain of Kent;" it is declared that he had taken upon himself royal power, and gathered to him the King's people in great number, "by false subtil imagined language," and had "seditiously made a stirring rebellion and insurrection under colour of justice, for the reformation of the laws of the King," robbing, slaying, and spoiling "great part of his faithful people:" and, thereupon, Cade was adjudged a traitor, and all indictments and acts done by him were declared void.

Robert Poynings, who was uncle of the Countess of Northumberland, and had acted as Cade's "Carver and Sewer," gave further evidence of the discontent. He was charged before Parliament with having, on the 26th February, 1453, sent letters

[1] Sussex Arch. Coll. xxi. p. 8.
[2] 31 Hen. VI. c. i.

and writings from Sutton, near Seaford, to Robert Poyntell of the same place, and John Cawe, of Lytyllyn, both "Husbondmen," (who had been indicted of High Treason against the King's person, when he was last at the city of Chichester, and had been pardoned,) to come to him, which they did on the last day of February, to Southwark, and with having given them money, thanked them for their good-will, and prayed them to be ready to come to him when he should give them warning. He was also charged with having, on the 20th of January, caused Thomas Bigg, of Lambeth, "yoman," outlawed of treason, and John Wildeley, of Southwark, and other riotous persons to have assembled at Westerham and caused a riot. He was thereupon summoned to appear in Chancery;[1] but evaded the summons by taking sanctuary in Westminster, and whilst there he was further charged with holding daily fellowship with those who had been indicted of felony and treason, and with having gone out when he would; and especially with having on the 15th, 16th, and 17th days of March, in 1454, at North Cray and Fremingham, and other places in Kent, ridden[2] in "riottes wyse, and arraied in manere of warre, that is to sey, with jackes, coats of mail, sallettes (helmets) and with other array of warre;" and it was thereupon ordained that he and his sureties should forfeit their recognizance.

Among the Miscellanea of the Exchequer is a writ dated 3rd June, 32 Hen. VI. (1454), commanding the Sheriff of Kent to seize the possessions of Robert Poynings esquire, and his sureties Thomas Hadres, William Hadley of Dartford yeoman, Richard Bolton of the same place yeoman, John Batall of Stanfield Ryvers in Essex esquire, John Bain of Dartford esquire, and Poynings' own brother Edward Poynings clerk, Master of Arundel College, forfeited under the Act.

"Joħes Robynson, Wiħs Bygge, Simon Morley, et Joħes Swayn, of the city of Canterbury.[4]

"Ričus Yonge, de *West⁹ham*, yoman, de hundɛ de WEST⁹HAM.

[1] Rot Parl. v. p. 396. [2] Ibid. p. 247 b.
[3] It is curious that Robert Poynings' son, Sir Edward Poynings, introduced the arbitrary "Poynings" law into Ireland. [4] Membrane 13.

"Wiłłs Norden et Georgius Colier, constabular' HUND⁹ DE TENAM; ac Wiłłs Aytheherst, de *Tenam*, yoman.

" Henr̄ Appelton, de Bukwell in parochia de *Boghton Aluph*, gentilman; Nicħus Godefelawe, de Boghton, yoman; Joħes Lane, de parochia de Boghton, yoman; Thomas Sabyne, de parochia de Boghton, yoman; Wiłłs Hely, de Boghton, husbondman; et Ric̄us Les, de parochia de Boghton, smith.

"Joħes Miller, de *Holyngbourne*, gentilman; Wiłłs Spert, de *Halden*, gentilman; Thomas Phclip, de *Ledes*, yoman; Joħes Norton, de *Stapleherst*, yoman; Joħes Morys, de *Holyngbourne*, laborer; Thomas Heron, de *Assheford*, laborer; Wiłłs Miller, de *Wrotham*, pulter; Robtus Miller, de *Wrotham*, pulter; Wiłłs Miller, de *Orpyngton*, husbondman; Ric̄us Miller, de *Cray b'e Marie*, pulter; and Thomas Miller, de *Orpyngton*, laborer; et alii.

" Laurencius Miller, de *Lenham;* et Ric̄us Miller, de *Lynstede*, yoman.

" Ric̄us Stydolf, de *Westerham*, mason; et Joħes atte Welle, de *Westerham*.

" Joħes Thorpe et Joħes Wybern, constabularij HUNDR⁹ DE WROTEHAM; ac Thomas Arcall; ac omnes alii hōes infra hundred predictam comorantes.

" Joħes Rowe de parochia de *Boxle;* Jacobus Burbage; Joħes Burbage; Henr̄ Dore; Robtus Burbage; Wiłł Rowe, de *Aylysford;* Edmundus Rowe, de *Aylysford;* et Hugo Wode, de *Rydyng.*

" Ric̄us Forthe, de *Strode*, yoman; Wiłłs Petur, et Joħes Northe de eadem.

" Joħes Colyer de *Mersham*, et Ric̄us Rolf de *Kyngyssnoth*, constabularii HUND' DE LANGEBREGGE; et Thomas Chapman, et omnes alii et singuli de hundredo predicto.

" Wiłłs Symon, de *Godm⁹sham*, et Dionisius Bakke, de *Chilham*, constabularii HUNDR⁹ DE FELBERGH; Nicħus Hylles, de *Godm⁹sham*, et omnes alii et singuli de hundr̄o et villa predictis.

" Wiłłs Foughyll, constabular̄ HUNDR' DE CHART, et Andreas Sprotte, et omnes alii, etc.

" Thomas Grymston, et Henr̄ Crompe, constabular̄ HUNDR' DE MOLTON; et Stepħus Waste, de *Stokebery;* ac omnes alii, etc.

"Johnes Godyng, constabularius VILLE DE TUNBRIGGE, yoman; Johes Partriche, de *Tunbrigge*, yoman; Johes Tyherst, senior, baker; Johes Huchyn, constabularius de HELDON, in parochia de *Tunbrigge;* et Johes Kypping, constabularius DE LA SOUTH BURGH, yoman; ac omnes alii, etc.

"Laurencius Mongeham, de parochia de *Stone;* et Henr̃ Dobyll, de *Wyttersham;* et omnes alii, etc., infra HUNDR' DE OXNEY commorantes.

"Johes Cheyne, de *Estchirche in Insula de Shephey*, miles, et Johes Symond, de *Mynstre* in Insula p̃dc̃a, husbondman; ac omnes alii, etc., infra insulam, etc.

"Goodmannus Durbarre, et Witts atte Towne, constabularij HUNDR' DE LANGPORTE; ac Thomas Bewefrere, de parochia de *Hope;* ac omnes, etc.

"Stephus Hogge, de parochia de *Frithynden*, gentilman, et Stephus Norton, de *Chart juxta Sutton*, gentilman; ac omnes alii de parochiis predictis.

"Johes Goolde, de *Middilton*, gentilman; Ric̃us Grouehirst, de eadem, gentilman; et Johes Buntyng, de eadem, gentilman.

"Henr̃ Cutbussh, de parochia de *Bydynden*, yoman; et Laurencius Heansell, de eadem, yoman; et omnes, etc., infra parochiam predictam.

"Johes Browne, ballivus VILLE DE FOLKSTON; ac omnes singuli, etc.

"Johes Ysaake, de *Patrykesbourne*, armig̃; et Witts Attewode, de *Brygge*, smyth; ac omnes, etc., infra HUNDRED' DE BRYGGE.

"Thomas Stobynbury, constabularius HUNDR' DE LYTELFELD; Witts Hexstall, de *Estpekham*, armig̃; Ric̃us Erkenbold; et Ric̃us Bake, de *Estpekham*, yoman; ac omnes alii, etc.

"Thomas Grene, de *Melton juxta Gravesende;* Thomas Ballyng, de *Gravesende*, husbondman; Thomas Plot, de Gravesende, yoman; et Johes Laurence, de Melton juxta Gravesende, yoman.

"Ric̃s Maye, de *Saundryssh,* ac omnes alii infra parochiam, etc.

"Johes Clerke,[1] de *Boughton Menchonse*, yoman; Robtus Meryhome, Henr̃ Hunt, ac Ric̃us Pikenden, ac omnes, etc.

[1] Memb. 12.

"Joñes Pastron, Joñes Welles, Ricus Shymyng, de parochia de *Boxle*, ac omnes alii, etc.

"Wiħs Fynne, de *Erith*, et Joñes Michell, de eadem; ac omnes alii, etc.

"Joñes Michell, de *Erith*, baker.

"Ricus Gildeford, de *Haukeherst*, taillour; Henr̃ Pelham, de Haukeherst, couper; Robtus Mercer, de Haukeherst, carpenter; Simon Pode, de Haukeherst, carpenter; et Joñes Frenshe, de Haukeherst, laborer; ac omnes alii, etc.

"Robtus Bernes, de Haukeherst, gentilman; Joñes Congeherst, de Haukeherst, gentilman; Joñes Watte, de Haukeherst, yoman; Robtus Stonden de Haukeherst, husbondman; Robtus Foutener, de Haukeherst, parish clerk; et Laurencius Heansell, de *Bydenden*, yoman; ac omnes alii, etc.

"Guido Attewode, de *Boughton Menchonse*, yoman; Wiħs Norton, de Boughton Menchonse; Thomas atte Wode; Henr̃ Purs; et Guido Gusing, de parochia de *Chilham*; ac omnes alii, etc.

"Joñes Roberd, de *Cranebroke*, senior, yoman; et Joñes Roberd, de Cranebrook, *junior*, gentilman; ac omnes alii, etc., de villa predicta.

"Joñes Tothe, de parochia de *Chipstede*, *junior*; Stepħus Tothe, de parochia de Chipstede; et Joñes Tommes, de parochia de Chepstede; ac omnes alii, etc.

"Thomas Changle, de Flete, in com̃ Lincolñ, alias dictus Thomas Changle, de *Ealdyng*, capellanus.

"Tħos Lawe, de Ealdyng, yoman; Robtus King, de Ealdyng, husbondman; Joñes Kyrbill, de Ealdyng, halywaterclerk; et Ricus Kyrbill, de Ealdyng, laborer.

"Wiħs Edward, de *Sandehurst*, gentilman; Tħos Heansell, de *Haukehurst*, yoman; Wiħs Bocher, de Haukeherst, smyth; et Thomas Mercer, de Haukeherst, repyer.

"Ricus Sankee, de *Seele*, yoman, ac omnes alii, etc.

"Thomas Heth, de *Woolwiche*, gentilman; et Ricus Lovelace, de *Byngesdom*, gentilman; ac omnes alii, etc.

"Wiħs Morecok; Tħos Morecok; Joñes Morecok; et Tħos Labe.

"Robtus Neyte; Thōs Bedmynton; Hugo Frere; et Wiłłs Bedmynton, de parochia de *Harytesgam*; as omnes alii, etc.

" Joħes Burbage, de *Buxle*, husbondman; Nicħus Faram, de eadem, husbondman; Ricūs Sebris, de eadem, mason; Joħes Joce de eadem, mason; Ricūs Manney, de *Maydeston*, mason; Robtus Burbage, de Boxle, laborer; Joħes Faram; Wiłłs Faram; et Joħes Bance.

" Robtus Nee, de parochia de *Heryotesham*; et Wiłłs Chamber; ac omnes alii, etc.

" Simon Shipton, de *Wolwiche*, yoman; Robtus Newdegate, de Woolwiche; et Wiłłs Pegge, de Woolwiche; ac omnes alii, etc.

" Wiłłs Northampton, de Wolwiche, gentilman; Thōs Attewode, de Wolwiche, husbondman; Joħes Edwyn, de Wolwiche, husbandman; Robtus Egell, de Wolwiche, boteman; Johes Frost, de Wolwiche, boteman; et Nicħus atte Gore, de Wolwiche, yoman; ac omnes alii, etc.

" Laurencius Engette, Joħes Grene, Joħes Crounber, Thomas Engette, Joħes Grouehurst, Wiłłs Colsall, Georgius Warman, Joħes Barker, Thomas Clement, Guido Withors, Wiłłs Lambert, et Joħes Harry, de parochia de *Ewade*, husbondmen; ac omnes, etc.

" Thomas Sprener, de *Melton juxta Gravesende*; Thomas Grene, de eadem; Thomas Wattys, de eadem, yoman; Joħes Page, de eadem, yoman; Joħes Hammes, de eadem, barbour; Robtus Hall, de eadem, laborer; Joħes Rede, de eadem, waƭman; Wiłłs Flour, de Gravesende, chaundeler; Thomas State, de Gravesende, yoman; Thomas Est, de Gravesende, haburdassher; Joħes Baker, de Gravesende, husbondman; Wiłłs Shene, de Gravesende, waƭman; et Wiłłs Fill, de Gravesende, carpenter.

" Thos. Happuldurfeld, de *Feversham*, armig̃; ac omnes alii, etc.

" Joħes Clerke, de *Kenordyngton*, husbondman; Thomas Benet; Joħes Spaget; Ricūs Bolte, cordewaner; Stepħus atte hille, husbondman; Joħes Miller, husbandman; Ricūs Andrewe, carpynter; Joħes Lyggand, carpenter; Ricūs Judde, husbondman; Ricūs Miller, cordewaner; Wiłłs Whiton, fyssher; Ricūs atte Rygge, husbondman; Wiłłs atte Reche, cordewaner; et Joħes Lucas, husbondman.

"Bernardus Cabell, de *Chesylherst*, husbondman, et Joħes Cabell, husbondman.

"Joħes Stanmer, de *Feversham*, yoman, *alias* dc̄us Joħes Davy, de eadem villa, yoman; cum hominibus ville predicte.

"Bartħus Bourne, de *Dodyngton*; Joħes Eytherst, de *Lyndestede*; Ric̄us Miller, de Lyndestede; Laurencius Roger, de Lyndestede; Joħes Cotyng, de eadem; Ric̄us Bedyll, de eadem; Joħes Dene, de eadem; Adam Grenestrete, de eadem; Wiłłs Marlere, de eadem; et Thomas Best, de eadem.

"Wiłłs Jole, de *Sundrysshe*.

"Wiłłs Mareys, de parochia de *Preston juxta Feuersham*, armig̃; ac omnes alii, etc.

"Waldus Waleys, de parochia de *Penshurst*, yoman; Wiłłs Warde, de parochia de *Havyr*, yoman, constabular̃ HUNDRED' DE SOM^{y}DEN; Thomas Wilbore, de parochia de *Chiddynston*; Joħes Clerk, de parochia de *Hevyr*, yoman; Joħes Broker, de parochia de *Chiddynston*, yoman; Rog^{9}us atte Wode, de parochia de Chiddyngston, yoman; Joħes Wodgate, de parochia de Chiddyngston, yoman; Wiłłs Ware, de parochia de Chiddyngston, yoman; Ric̄us Clerk, de parochia de Chiddyngston, yoman; Wiłłs Clerk, de parochia de Chiddyngston, yoman; Joħes Coret, de parochia de *Hevyr*, et Wiłłs Wymbyll, de parochia de *Hebyr*, yoman; ac omnes alii, etc.

"Wiłłs Edward, de *Sandeherst*, armig̃; Thomas White, de *Sandeherst*, husbondman, et Rob̃tus Bernes, de *Haukhirst*, gentylman;[1] ac omnes alii, etc.

"Laurencius Pakke et Rob̃tus Rows, ac omnes alij infra parochiam de *Barmynge*; ac Joħes Tutsam, Ric̄us Tutsam, Joħes Reve, et Wiłłs Hunt, ac omnes alii infra parochiam de *Westfarlegh*; Stepħus Crouche, ac omnes alii infra parochiam de *Watryng*; Ric̄us Baker, ac omnes alii infra parochiam de *Pekham*; necnon Joħes Crompe, Joħes Pakke senior, Joħes Pakke junior, Joħes Myller, Joħes Southland, Wiłłs Gore, Joħes Gore, Wiłłs

[1] See *ante* p. 43.

Kenelyn, Joħes Reve, Joħes Porter, Joħes Clyffe, Thomas Nasshe, et Joħes Hamond; ac omnes, &c.

"Thōs Hunte, et Pħus Castell, constabulaȓ HUNDR' DE FOLKESTON; ac Joħes Grenford, Wiħs Fyneux, et Nicħus Everynge; ac omnes alii, etc.

"Joħes Halke, constabulaȓ HUND' DE PETHAM; ac Thomas Bowll, et Simon Court; ac omnes alii, etc.

"Ricūs King, de *Cowlyng*, husbondman, constabulaȓ de HUND' DE SHANNILL; Henȓ Spencer, capellanus ecctie de Cowling; Joħes Pardour, de eadem; et Rogerus Smyth, de eadem, husbondman; ac omnes alii, etc.

"Roƀtus Ball, de *Thornham*, gentilman; Wiħs Lorde, de *Berghstede*, bocher; Hermanus Pokill, de Berghstede, draper; Joħes Wenyall, de Berghstede, ripier; Joħes Reynold, de *Ledys*, bocher; Thōs Reynold, de Ledys, bocher; Roƀtus Wodegate, de Ledys, husbondman; Wiħs Everynden, de Ledys, husbondman; Georgius Lovynden, de *Holyngbourne*, fuller; Ricūs Peny, de Holyngbourne, laborer; Joħes Adam, de Holyngbourne, corveser; Joħes Ayot, de Holyngbourne, senior, husbondman; Joħes Broke, de Holyngbourne, husbondman; Joħes Lambe, de Holyngbourne, husbondman; Wiħs Fox, de Holyngbourne, laborer; Roƀtus Gybbys, de Holyngbourne, draper; Wiħs Breche, de Holyngbourne, draper; Roƀtus atte Wode, de Holyngbourne, husbondman; Roƀtus Paulyn, de Holyngbourne, laborer; Gilƀtus Bresyng, de Holyngbourne, laborer; Roƀtus Isowede, de Holyngbourne, laborer; Joħes Tayllour, de Holyngbourne, husbondman; Thomas Charlys, de Holyngbourne, laborer; Thomas Halk, de Holyngbourne, fuller; et Simon Halk, de Holyngbourne, carpenter; ac omnes alii, etc.

"Rog^{y}us Stede, de *Heryettesham*, repyer.

"Joħes Mason, de *Maydeston*, wexchaundeler.

"Joħes Cattys, de *Wroteham*, gentylman; Thomas Chapman, de eadem, yoman; Joħes Barbour, de eadem, yoman; Joħes Whyte, de eadem, yoman; Stepħus Wrange, de eadem, yoman; Ricūs Benet, de eadem, yoman; Joħes at Well, de eadem, yoman; Joħes Sexteyn, de eadem, yoman; Thomas Wryght, de eadem, yoman; Thomas Arcell, de eadem, yoman; Johes Hunte, de eadem, yoman; et Johes Palgrave, de eadem, yoman.

"Wilts Belde, de *Cantuar'*, gentilman.

"Johes Penwortham, de *Cantuar'*, gentilman.

"Thomas Andrewe, de *Dertford*, sondeer, *alias* baker, *alias* newbaker.

"Thomas Stokyngbury, smyth; Thomas Partiche, smyth; John Koos, husbondman; Wilts Knocher, de *Estpekham*, smyth.

Johes Clerk, psona *eccl'ie de Halgeste*, in HUN' DE HES ;[1] Stephus Nelyr et Johes Turner, constabularij ejusdem hundr'; ac omnes alii, etc.

"Rog²us Cheseman, de Eltham, et Edmundus Ryculff, de Lee, constabularius HUND' DE BLAKEHETH ; ac omnes alii, etc.

"Thomas Pympe, de parochia *Omnium Sanctorum* infra HUND' DE HOO, et Johes Turnour, constabularius hund p̄dc̄i; ac omnes alii, etc., infra villam.

"Thomas atte Wode, de *Northflete*, smyth; Ricus Longfeld, de eadem, senior, husbondman; Ricus Somer, de eadem, fyssher; Johes Addys, de eadem, laborer ; Wilts Parke, de eadem, carpenter; Thomas Fluke, de eadem, husbondman; Ricus Hauker, de eadem, husbondman ; Johes Hull, de eadem, husbondman ; Wilts Edwyn, de eadem, haly waterclerk; Wilts Ingram, de eadem, husbondman ; Danielus Longfeld, de eadem, husbondman; Simon Letot, de eadem, husbondman ; Ricus Letot, de eadem, notery ; Ricus Gervays, de eadem, husbondman ; Wilts de Roy, de eadem, husbondman; Wilts Kyng, de eadem, husbondman ; Johes Garred, de eadem, husbondman ; Thomas Gold, de eadem, husbondman ; Wilts Smyth, de eadem, husbondman ; Johes Leveshot, de eadem, husbondman; Stephus Shadde, de eadem, husbondman; Henr̄ Dyker, de eadem, laborer; Ricus Goldger, de eadem, laborer ; Ricus Tyler, de eadem, tyler ; Ricus Longvyle, de eadem, junior, husbondman ; Johes Harlowe, de eadem, husbondman; Robtus Harlowe, de eadem, husbondman ; Johes Dyne, de eadem, husbondman ; Johes Pers, de eadem, husbondman; et Johes Wright, de eadem, husbondman.

"Johes Martyn, de *Dertford*, gentilman, alias Johes Martyn

[1] Membrane 11.

nuper de *Quaplodin com' Lincoln'*, gentilman; Wfts Rotheley, de Dertford, yoman; Rog͡us Rotbeley, de eadem, yoman; Robtus Aleyn, de eadem, gentilman; et Walterus Groveherst, de eadem, gentilman.

" Johes Rowe, of *Boxle*, gentilman; Robtus Rowe, of *Aillsford*, gentilman; Wfts Rowe, of Aillsford, gentilman; Robtus Rowe, of Aillesford, gentilman; Henry Dore, de *Boxle;* Jacobus Burbage, de Boxle; Johes Burbage, de Boxle; Robtus Burbage, de Boxle, yoman; et Hugo Wode, de *Ealdyng*, gentilman; ac omnes alii, etc.

" Robtus Somercy, de *Stapulherst*, gentilman; Stephus Hernden, de eadem, husbondman; Johes Exherst, de eadem, husbondman; Thomas Enghurst, de eadem, barbour; Johes Berman, de eadem, husbondman; Thomas . . . . . ,[1] de eadem, laborer; Thomas Benryng, de eadem, husbondman; et Ricus Moys, de eadem, husbondman; ac omnibus, etc.

" Wftis Lovelace, alias Lovelas, de Merton, in com. Surr., alias dc̄us Wfts nup. de *Betrysden*, gentilman.

" Johes Burwessh, de *Guyfford*, yoman.

" Johes Elys, de *Octham*, gentilman; Wfts Colyn, de eadem, yoman; Thomas atte Hatche, de eadem, bocher; Walt͡us Lovell, de parochia de *Langle*, yoman.

" Rog͡us Yong, de HUNDR' DE WESTRAM.

" Ricus Sabyn, constabularius HUNDR' DE MADESTON; Johes Colncy, de eadem; Wfts Bele, de eadem.

" Wfts Symond et Dionisius Bak, constabular. hundr̃ de FELBERGH;[2] ac omnes alii, etc.

" Wfts Kayem *alias* dictus Roule, de parochia de *Bradgare;* Henr̃ Crumpe, de eadem; Phus Sayer, de eadem; Elias Bocher, de eadem; Wfts Frensh, de eadem; Thomas Breggeham, de eadem; Elias Breggeham, de eadem; Thomas Drury, de eadem; Robtus Drury, de eadem; Wfts Grenehell, de eadem; Elias Grenehell, de eadem; Johes Couper, de eadem; Johes Castell, de eadem; Wfts Heneger, de eadem; Ricus Canon, de eadem; Wfts Lather, de eadem; et Petrus Premer, de eadem.

" Ricus Yonge, de *Westerham*.

[1] *Sic.* [2] See *ante* p. 41.

JOHN CADE'S FOLLOWERS IN KENT. 49

"Rog̃us Twysden, de *Magna Chart*, gentilman; et Joħes Gybbes, de eadem, gentilman.

" Wiħs Chaundellar et Riĉus Carter, constabularij HUNDR' DE COTESHECHE ; ac omnes et singuli, etc.

" Dionisius Buttur et Joħes Simons, constabularij HUNDR' DE FELBAROGH ; Wiħs Petet, Bartħus Dryland, Roƀtus Godebarn, et Nicħus Hylles ;[1] ac omnes alii, etc.

" Joħes Fyssher, de *Maydeston*, carpenter; Joħes Bird, de *Clynton;* Jacobus Hope, de *Wyngham,* gentilman : ac Joħes Oxenden, de Wyngham, gentilman; ac Jacobus Cluterynden et Riĉus Pury, constabularii HUNDR' DE WYNGHAM ; ac omnes, etc.

" Wiħs Haute, armig̃, Riĉus Mynot, et Joħes Denne, ac omnes, etc., infra HUNDR' DE KYNGHANFORD.

" Walt̃us Waleys et Wiħs Warde, constabularij HUNDR' DE SOM̃DEN ;[2] Thomas Wilbore, de *parochia de Chiddyngston*, yoman; Joħes Broker, de eadem, yoman; Rog̃us atte Wode, de eadem, yoman; Joħes Wodgate, de eadem, yoman; Wiħs Ware, de eadem, yoman; Riĉus Clerk, de eadem, yoman; Wiħs Clerk, de eadem, yoman; Wiħs Hunt, de eadem, yoman ; Joħes Clerk, de parochia de *Hebyr*, yoman ; Joħes Coret, de eadem, yoman ; et Wiħs Wymbyll, de eadem, yoman; ac omnes, etc.

" Simon Benet et Thomas Mantell, constabular̃ HUNDR' DE BOUGHTON ATTE BLENNE ; et Thomas Burgeys, et Roƀtus Drylond; ac omnes, etc.

" Riĉus Walshe et Bernardus Cabell, constabularij HUNDR' DE ROKESLE, ac Joħes Mager, Pħus atte Welle, Riĉus Maynard, Joħes Bertlotte, et Wiħs Rowe, ac omnes, etc.

" Joħes Mortymer, ac Wiħs Foule, de *Westwykham*, husbondman ; Thomas Wodeward, de Westwykham, husbondman; Wiħs Aleyn, de Westwykham, husbondman; et Thomas Stone, de parochia de Westwykham, husbondman; ac omnes alii, etc.

" Hugo Chedyngston, de *Sundrisshe;* Joħes Style, de parochia de Sundrisshe; et Thomas Baker, de eadem, clerk; ac omnes alii, etc.

[1] See *ante*, pp. 41, 42.   [2] See *ante*, p. 45.

JOHN CADE'S FOLLOWERS IN KENT.

"Thomas Henere; Robtus Seylyard; Johes Seylyerd; Johes Josewey; Thomas Chaunceler; Johes Bardog; Willis Colman; Johes Slyghtre; Ricus Oughtrede; Rogus Wodewarde; Ricus Swon; Johes Swon, fil ejus; Johes Fychet; Ricus Fychet; Ricus Ware; Johes Chepstede, junior; Thomas Chelscombe; Willis Twyford; Johes Rouland; et Johes Ganyll; ac omnes, etc.

"Willis Menhome; Johes Whillok; Johes Lenenorth, de *Broughton Menchonse;* Johes Herynden et Johes Tempulmarche; ac omnes, etc.

"Thomas Reme, de *Renham,* gentilman.

"Petrus Pedynden, de *Borden,* husbondman; et Ricus Capron, de eadem, husbondman; ac omnes, etc.

"Johes Richyngood, de *Kingesloue infra Insula de Thanet:* ac omnes, etc.

"Thomas Wclde, constabularius[1] VILLE DE BRASTEDE et LUCATE DE TUNBRIGGE; Robtus Parker; Thomas Crowe; Johes Harry; Nichus Dore; Ricus Harry; Robtus Harry; Georgius Jurdayn; Willis atte Meer; Thomas Lake; Johes Brightrede; Johes Swan, drover; et Ricus Pakke; ac omnes alii, etc.

"Robtus Clyfton, de parochia de *Clyfton,* gentilman; Johes Bocher, de *Barmesey,* yoman; Ricus Martyndale, yoman; et Ricus Broun, de eadem, yoman.

"Johes Nassh, de *Merden,* yoman; Johes Rolf, de eadem, yoman; ac omnes, etc.

"Willis Norton, de parochia de *Sheldwych,* gentilman; ac omnes, etc.

"Johes Fraunceys, subconstabularius de *Estgate* in parochia *S'd Nichi in suburbio de* ROUCHESTRE; ac omnes, etc.

"Johes Gerold, de parochia *S'c'e Margarete in suburbio de Rouchestre,* husbondman; ac omnes, etc.

"Johes Bornman, Johes fil Johis Bornman, Ricus Bornman, Stephus Bornman, et Jacobus Bornman, de parochia de *Boughton Menchonse;* ac omnes alii, etc.

"Robtus Mertyn, de *Wye;* Johes Rosc; Willis London; Thomas Wyllok, et Johes Ourle, de Wye; ac omnes, etc.

[1] Membrane 10.

JOHN CADE'S FOLLOWERS IN KENT.

"Joħes Godyng, de *Estpekham*, yoman; Joħes Esthawe, de Estpekham, yoman; Robtus Colyn, de Estpekham, smyth; et Wiłłs Godyng, de Estpekham, yoman, constabularij HUND' DE LYTTELFELD; ac omnes etc.

"Ričus Forde, de parochia de *Penseherst*, gentilman; ac omnes, etc.

" Joħes Kyrkkwode, Ričus Byrdemere, et Joħes Tysedale.

" Joħes Gulby, de *Dertford*; Robtus Barbour, de eadem; Joħes Herde, de eadem; Joħes Freeman, de eadem; Joħes de Dene, de eadem; et Henř Serman, de eadem, ac omnes, etc., de *Stoneham, Mershstrete*, et *Stoneheld*, ac de parochia de *Dertford*.

" Ničus Champeneys, Ričus Edlyn, Joħes atte Nobyn, Thomas Gylbe, Joħes Mason, Joħes Stokke, Joħes Sandyr, Ričus Frere, Simon Boydon, Ričus Alcote, Joħes Coryour, Thomas Hencote senior, Thomas Hencote junior, Thomas atte Nobyn, Joħes Alcote, Joħes North, Joħes Ely, Wiłłs Copedyll, Henř Tenaker, Thomas Couper senior, Joħes Adam, Thomas Kyng, Joħes Capell, Joħes Archer, Joħes Thomson, Wiłłs Yonge, Ričus Auncell, Joħes Clerk, Ričus Harbard, Gilbtus Harbard, Wiłłs Harbard, Wiłłs Carpynter, Joħes Abbotte, Ričus Jordan, Rog^{9}us Couper, Gerardus Wangystell, Joħes Nebman, Joħes Herte, Wiłłs Palmer, et Thomas Pesok, de parochia de *Strode*, ac omnes, etc.

" Thomas Deynold, de *Cantuar*; Joħes Garwynton, Wiłłs Bele, Rog^{9}us Toly, Ričus Carpenter, Ričus Upton, Joħes Bate, et Joħes Beke, de eadem, ac omnes alii et singuli de eadem civitate.

" Wiłłs Lorde, de *Berstede*, bocher, Hermanus Pokell, de eadem, draper; Simon Meller, de eadem, mason; Robtus Heynes, de eadem, husbondman; Pħus Joce, de eadem, carpenter; Joħes Coker, de eadem, husbondman; Rog^{9}us Edward de eadem, husbondman; Wiłłs Carter, de eadem, yoman; Henř Brewer, de eadem, mason; Andreas Gardener, de eadem, mason; Simon Coker, de eadem, mason; Robtus Style, de eadem, mason; Thomas Rokesacre, de eadem, mason; Ričus Clerk, de eadem, barbour; Joħes William, de eadem, webbe; et Joħes Hopkyn, de eadem, husbondman.

"Johes Chamberleyn, alias Johes Smethcote, de *Estfarle*, gentilman.

"Johes Boteler, de *Boughton Malherbe*, cticus: Wihs Clerk, de eadem, senior, husbondman ; Wihs Clerk, de eadem, junior, husbondman; Henr̃ Swerenden, de eadem; Thomas Wylkyns, de eadem, laborer; Johes Allyn, de eadem, husbondman; Johes Hooker, de eadem, husbondman; Johes Coveney, de eadem, laborer; Johes Tyler, de eadem, tyler ; Henr̃ Cook, de eadem, wever ; Galfrid Brodeway, laborer; Johes Sednour, de eadem, husbondman; Wihs Stonehous, de eadem, husbondman ; Johes Stonehous, de eadem, husbondman; Johes Stenhous, de eadem, sexteyn : Johes Hasylwode, de eadem, husbondman; et Johes Rogger, de eadem, husbondman; ac omnes, etc.

"Ričus Coyff, de *Speldehurst*, husbondman; Johes Crudde, de eadem, yoman; Ričus Crudde, de Penshurst, yoman; et Nichus Crundewell, de eadem, yoman.

"Walthus Waleys, de *Penshurst*, yoman; Thomas Berkele, de eadem, yoman; Wihs Peyntour, de *Chidyngston*, husbondman ; Johes Basset, de eadem, yoman; Wihs Harlakenden, de *Wodechurche*, yoman; Wihs Clerk, de eadem, yoman; et Alanus Engeham, de eadem, yoman.

"Walthus Langley, de HUNDR' DE ESTRY, gentilman, ac omnes, etc.

"Wihs Wynterbourne de *Esthetisford*, alias de *Wy*, gentilman; et Ričus Dodyston, de *Westwelle*.

"Johes Gerveys, de parochia de *Zele*.

"Johes Stone, junior, gentilman, ac omnes, etc.

"Thomas Swyst, de *Sandewico*, yoman; et Thomas Stokes, yoman.

"Johes Cosyn, de *Cantuar*', grocer.

"Thomas Chelscombe, de *Sundrysshe*.

"Thomas Reculuer, constabularius HUND' DE CHATEHAM;[1] Wihs Covler, Johes Covler, Ričus Covler, Hamo Covler, Thomas Friday, Wihs Thorp senior, Johes Thorp senior, Johes Thorp junior, Johes Smyth, Thomas Smyth, Rog^{9}us atte Wode, Wihs Warner, Thomas Warner, Johes Symcok, Ričus Lorkyn, Ričus

[1] Membrane 9.

JOHN CADE'S FOLLOWERS IN KENT.

Cristyan, Rog͡us Roper, Stepħus Cok, Joħes Cok, Simon Couper, Robtus Wodear, Ricus Bedmynton, Witts Short, Witts Neel junior, Joħes Pylcher, Witts Pylcher, Joħes Chapman, Ricus Marchall, Joħes Wolf, Witts Neel senior, Joħes Tomme, Thomas Pery senior, Thomas Pery junior, Joħes Pery, bocher, Hamo Long, Witts Long, Joħes Pylcher, Robtus Chelfeld, Ricus Long, Thomas Long, ac Robtus Godfray, constabularius HUNDR' DE GYLLYNGHAM; Joħes Broun, Thomas Pery, Joħes Mylle, Witts Mylle, Joħes Dygon, Joħes Keneworth, Michael Gybhe, Joħes Harry, Thomas Davy, Thomas Acton, Joħes Ram, Witts Grenehill senior, Ricus Rogger, Witts Grenehill junior, Ricus Bery, et Stepħus Heyward, bocher, de paroch de *Chatteham, Gillyngham*, et *Grean*.

" Witts Pery, de parochia de *Gyllyngham*, ac omnes, etc.

" Thōs Edolff, de *Westmallyng*, yoman, ac omnes alii, etc.

" Joħes Shepherd, de *Bromley*, husbondman; et Witts Shepherd, de Bromley, husbondman.

" Witts Harry, de *Est Gate*, in parochia S'c'i Nich'i, in suburbio de *Rouchestre*, bruer, ac omnes, etc.

" Joħes Drury, de *Sandewico*, armig̃.

" Joħes Fyneux, armig̃.

" Witts Symond et Dionisius Bak, constabulaī HUND' DE FELBERGH,[1] ac omnes, etc.

" Joħes Duke, Jacobus atte Forde, Joħes Smythest senior, Joħes Rolf, Joħes Bechyng, Robtus Kent, Joħes Badisden, Ricus Bechyng, et Stepħus Capell, de *Haukeherst*, ac omnibus, etc.

" Joħes Paston, de *Sandewico*, bocher.

" Pħus Aleysaunder, Robtus Davie, Robtus Rose, Thomas Fytyll, Witts Caweston, Ricus Pyknote, Joħes Dawe, Joħes Umfrey, Robtus Langley, Ricus Langley, Thomas Dawe, Joħes Halston, Joħes Kyng, Joħes Beton, Witts Plege, Joħes Aylcmer, Joħes Whode, Radus Mason, et Joħes John, seruantelaugge, de parochia de *Bekynham*.

" Thomas Thornton, de *Gravesend*, hakeneyman; et Witts Fyll, de eadem, carpenter.

" Robtus Berlond, de *Reynham*, yoman; Ricus Renell, de

[1] See *ante*, pp. 45, 49.

eadem, husbondman ; Johes Chaunterell, de eadem, husbondman ; Stephus Aymer, de eadem, husbondman ; Johes Symond, de eadem, husbondman ; Johes Walware, de eadem, husbondman ; Willhs Christian, de eadem, husbondman ; et Willhs Whitle, de eadem, husbondman.

"Robtus Cheseman, et Thomas Cheseman, de *Estgrenewich*, ac omnes, etc.

"Simon Vaghen, de *Gravesend*, gentilman ; Ričus Plotte, de Gravesend, shipman ; Johes Merssho, de Gravesend, maryner ; Johes Plotte, de Gravesende, maryner; Thomas Hardy, de Gravesende, maryner; Thomas Plotte, de Gravesende, junior, maryner ; Willhs Hardy, de Gravesende, maryner ; Willhs Wodestocke, de Gravesend, maryner ; Johes Feryer, de Gravesende, bargeman; et Thomas Gwyn, de Gravesende, maryner, ac omnes, etc.

"Johes Bokynfold, de *Upcherch*, yoman; Johes Clement, de *Newenton* husbondman ; et Thomas Longe, de Newynton, husbondman.

"Willhs Sclowe, de *Cantuar'*, mercer ; et Johes Fermyngham, de Cantuar, bocher.

"Johes Baker, de *Maydeston*, yoman.

"Johes Ildergate, de *Sandewich*, armig⁰.

"Edmundus Chertesey, de *Rouchestre*, gentilman ; et Ričus Culpepyr, nuper de *Estfarlegh*, gentilman.

"Thomas Cardon, de *Clyve*, gent; Johes Cardon, de eadem ; gent; Laurencius Mundyn, de eadem, shipman; Ričus Mepham, de eadem, chaundeler ; et Thomas Mepham, de eadem, husbondman.

"Walt⁰us Crepegge, de *Denton*, husbondman; et Johes Martyn, de *Chalk*, husbondman.

"Johes Potkyn, de *Chalke*, senior, husbondman ; et Johes Potkyn, de eadem, junior, husbondman.

"Johes Cokke, de Borstall, in parochia de *Plumstede*, yoman; et Thomas Pycard, de parochia de *Grehithe*, yoman, constabularii HUNDR' DE LYTLE et LESON, ac omnes, etc.

"Stephus Colvey, de *Maydeston*, goldsmyth, ac omnes, etc.

"Willhs Fynche, de Maydeston, taillour, ac omnes, etc.

JOHN CADE'S FOLLOWERS IN KENT.

" Wiħs Edericbe, de *Estgrenewich*, et Alicia, ux ejus; Rog̅ʹus Cokke, de Estgrenewiche; Henr̃ Newerk, de Estgrenewiche, et Margareta, ux ejus; Joħes Brambill, de Estgrenewiche, et Alicia, ux ejus.

" Ric̃us Snelgorre, de *Boxley*, yoman, ac omnes, etc.

" Joħes Newenham, de *Strode*, yoman;[1] et Ric̃us Broke, de *Rouchestre*, yoman, ac omnes.

" Robtus Chamberleyn, de *Merworth*; et Joħes Chamberleyn, de parochia de *Lose*.

" Robtus Est, de *Maydeston*, gentilman.

" Jacobus Scheterynden et Joħes Pery, constabularii de HUNDR' de WYNGHAM, ac Joħes Oxenden et Wiħs Donyngton, ac omnes, etc.

" Wiħs Wodhell, constabular̃ HUNDR' de PRESTON, ac Joħes Halle, et Joħes Rekedon, et omnes, etc.

" Ric̃us Hervy et Joħes Downe, constabular̃ de HUŇD' DE ESTRY, ac Joħes Chamberleyn, et Thomas Roger, ac omnes, etc.

" Joħes Cokke, de Borstall, in parochia de *Plumstede*, yoman; Joħes Crabbe, de Borstall, in parochia de Plumstede, yoman; Radus Yonge, de Borstall, yoman; Robtus Ricard, de parochia de Plumstede, maryner; Edmundus atte Wode, de parochia de *Erehithe*, yoman; Thomas Jonson, Ric̃us Jonson, Rog̅ʹus Rodley, Joħcs Forger, Joħes Hychecok, Joħes Bolton, de parochia de Erehithe; Robtus Drynker, de parochia de *Plumstede*; et Galfr̃us Herte, de *Creyford*, yoman.

" Joħes Crouche, de *Milton*, husbondman; et Wiħs Bull, de eadem, husbondman.

" Ric̃us Adam, de *parva Charte*, yoman.

" Thomas Ballard, de parochia de *Estgrenewyche*, armiger; Joħes Shamele, Wiħs More, Joħcs Sharpe, Wiħs Hanford, Robtus Aytan, Robtus Turnour, et Joħes Pyers, de eadem parochia; ac Ric̃us Hunte, de parochia de *Charteham*; Thomas Andrewe, de eadem; Thomas Lynsey, de eadem; Thomas Osmere, de *Est Sutton*; Pħus Joce, de parochia de *Melton*; et Adam Boke, de *Petham*.

" Jacobus Grandon et Thomas Boorne, de parochia de *Hithe*.

[1] Membrane 8.

"Witts Serle, de parochia de *Chevenyng* de Chepestede, yoman; et Witts Sharp, de eadem parochia, yoman.

" Johes Notyngham, de parochia de *Herne*, yoman; et Johes att Chirch, alias Cherch, de eadem parochia, yoman.

" Robtus Payn, de *Bekenham*, husbondman;[1] et Andreas Wodecock, de *Bromley*, husbondman, constabularij HUND' DE BROMLEY et BEKENAM.

" Johes Bolt, de parochia de *Pensherst*,[2] husbondman; John Hert, husbondman; Johes Grombrigge, husb.; Thomas Godeyere, husb.; Walt⁹us Beche, de Pensherst, senior, husb.[3]; Nichus Crondewell, husb.; Johes Roger, husb.; Johes Holt, husb.; Nichus Holt, husb.; Walt⁹us Beche, husb.; Walt⁹us Waleys, yoman; Ričus Hamond, bocher, Johes Bulman, gent,[4] Thomas Fuller, husb.; Ričus Fuller, husb. de Penherst; Johes Wodegate, de *Chedyngstone*, senior, husb.; Johes Wodegate, junior, husb.; Johes Sleyghter, husb.; Johes Basset, de Chedyngstone, husbondman; Johes Crudde, de *Speldherst*, husbondman; Witts Crudde, de Speldherst, husb.; et Witts Sakery, de Speldherst, ac omnes alii, etc.

" Johes Norton, Thomas Sadyer, Johes Grangeman, Thomas Godwat, Witts Peny, Petrus Breggeham, Ričus Tomlyn, Thōs Dane, Witts Dylot, Ričus Storey, Witts Storey, Elias Ladde, Witts Louce, Henr̄ Storey, Robtus Strangbowe senior, Walt⁹us Coke, Elias Loosmyth, Witts Catelot, Robtus Loosmyth, Johes Loosmyth senior, Witts Strangbowe, Witts Barlyng, Benedcus Geley, Johes Holman senior, Johes Coke, Johes Tomlyn, Henr̄ Rere, Ričus Caperon, Robtus Strangbowe junior, Johes Strangbowe, Johes Lowe, Robtus Lowe, Johes Loosmyth junior, Henr̄ Kyryell, Ričus Roger, Thomas Tomlyn, Johes Bedell, Petrus Petynden, Witts Mowere, Witts Jan, Johes Lydsyng, Thomas Clenche, Barthus Plotte, Johes Lovedere, Thomas Heystede, Robtus Knyghtō, Johes Gygman, et Stephus Dane, de parochia de *Borden*, ac omnes, etc.

" Robtus Rogger, de *Lenham*, yoman; Johes Colyare, yoman;

---

[1] Membrane 7.
[2] Penshurst then belonged to Humphrey Stafford, Duke of Buckingham.
[3] Where husb. is printed the word is at length in the original.
[4] So also gent.

Johes Bysshop, de eadem, tailour; Johes Bakere, de eadem, bakere; Witts Gybbe, de eadem, tanner; Johes Gybbe, de eadem, tanner; et Safirus Couper, de eadem, cowper, ac omnes, etc.

" Ričus Kelshale, de *Holyngbourne*, husbondman; Johes Tylare, de eadem, taillour; et Witts Filcote, de eadem, husbondman.

" Robtus Perry, trumpet.

" Thomas Tragosse, de *Boorghley*, gent.

" Witts Odyerne, de *Wittresham*, in hundr' de Oxene, gent.; Jacobus Glover, yeoman; Laurencius Taillour, yoman; Witts Budde, yoman; Augustinus Potyn, yoman; Witts Aas, yoman; Witts Austyn, yoman; Johes Jolyf, husb.; Johes Mapysden, yoman; Jacobus Mapysden, yoman; Witts Browenyng, husb.; Jacobus Huberd, yoman; Thomas Godfrey, yoman; Johes Warner, husbondman; Johes Potyn, yoman; Johes Glover, yoman; Witts Morleyn, husb.; Witts Potyn, husb.; Johes Chyboll, husb.; Stephus Boydon, husb.; et Stephus Sexteyn, de Wittresham, husbondman.

"Nichus Trendehorst, de parochia de *Lyde*, yoman.

" Thomas Harry, de *Halden*, draper; Witts Fox, de *Mersham*, yoman.

" Johes Hughlyn, de *Ossechurche*, yoman; Johes Kempe, de *Romaney*, yoman; Ričus Heed, de *Snergate*, yoman; Thomas Heed, de eadem; et Johes Adam, de *Brokelond*, wever.

"Johes Osbern, de *Trottesclyff*, yoman; Ričus Chaunceler, de eadem, husbondman; Johes Tenere, de eadem, husbondman; Robtus Symcok, de eadem, husbondman; Ričus Rous, de eadem, husb.; Johes Cheseman, de eadem, taillour; Thomas Osbern, de eadem, laborer; et Johes William, de eadem, husbondman; ac omnes, etc.

" Henř Cutbusshe, de *Bedynden*, yoman, qui se sicut p̃fert eidem Johi Mortymer.

" Johes Baker, de *Maydeston*, yoman qui se sicut p̃fert eidem Johi Mortymer.

" Thomas Smyth, de *Ealdyng*, yoman; Johes Goldsmyth, de

Ealding, yoman; et Wiłłs Goldsmyth, de *Hincton*, yoman, ac omnes, etc.

" Johes Burgoyne, qui se sicut p̃fert eidem Joħi Mortymer.

" Johes Pepysham, de *Goodherst*, laborer; Robtus Rye, de *Coumbewell*, laborer; Johes Tregge, de *Flemynwell*, husb.; Johes Courthope, de Flemynwell, husb.; Robtus Jurdan, de *Hangherst*, husbondman; Thomas Jurdan, de *Goodherst*, husb.; Wiłłs Muggc, de Goodherste, rypyer; Thomas Mugge, de Goodherst, rypyer; Johes Norton, de Goodherst, corveser; Rogus Smyth, de Goodherst, laborer; Sp̄hus Berworth, de Goodherst, laborer; et Thomas Berworth, de Goodherst, yoman, ac omnes, etc.

" Johes Mulling, de *Cantuar*'; Johes Wynter, de Cantuar̄; Thomas Proude, de Cantuar̄; Wiłłs Sellowe, de Cantuar̄, mercer; Johes Harnhill, de Cantuar̄; Radus Sutton, Johes Sutton, Ric̄us Barnes, de Cantuar̄, brasyer; et Wiłłs Bryan, ac omnes, etc.

" Rogus Ridlee, de Cantuar̄, gent.; Johes Newerk; Ric̄us Pargate, de Cantuar̄; Ric̄us Munden, de eadem; et Ric̄us Newerk, ac omnes, etc.

" Laurencius Stonestrete, Nicħus Bulbroke, Johes Cotyng, Wiłłs Sprynget, Johes Polyner, Robtus Wykern, Laurencius Gerad, Nicħus Bokyngham, Johes Underdowne, Thomas Baskenyle, Laurencius Lovell, Robtus Taillour, Johes Myles, de *Sydyngburn*; Simon Sylk, Thomas Pers, Johes Beche, Johes Baker, Wiłłs Denwey, Nicħus Graungeman, et Johes Loksmyth.

" Wiłłs Ayott, de parochia de *Holyngburn*, yoman.

" Johes Buttet, de *Brounley*, husb., alias Jenyns Buttet.

" Walt̃us Culpepyr, de *Gouteherst*, armig.; Johes Culpepyr, de eadem, fił ejus; Ric̄us Culpepyr; Wiłłs Foule; Thomas Sancok; Thomas Wychynden; et Ric̄us Moyes, ac omnes alii, etc.

" Johes Culpepyr, de *Gouteherst*, gent; Wiłłs Muggc, de eadem; Johes Love, de eadem; Johes Bace, de eadem; Sp̄hus Love, de eadem; Johes Benke, de eadem; Johes Baldok, de eadem; Thomas Dorley, de eadem; Thomas Wayte, de eadem; Johes Patyndon, de eadem; Johes Baker, de eadem; et Ric̄us Streter, de eadem, et omnes, etc.

JOHN CADE'S FOLLOWERS IN KENT. 59

"Joĥes Yorke, alias Joĥes Kelyng, de parochia de *Bekenam*, senior, husb.; Joĥes de Yorke, alias Joĥes Kelyng, de parochia de Bekenam, husbondman; Joĥes Middey, de parochia de Bekenam, husb.; et Wiĥs Middey, de parochia de Bekenam, husb., et in hunđ de Bromeley et Bekenam, ac omnes, etc.

"Joĥes Gylford, de *Dolling*, gentilman.

"Joĥes atte Water, Galfr̃us Breknok, Thomas Stranbowe, Thomas Hogyn, de parochia de *Bobbyng*, ac omnes, etc.

"Wiĥs Sprynget, de *Sedyngburn*, yoman; Laurencius Lovell, de eadem; Joĥes Quynte, de eadem; Joĥes Norden, de eadem; et Joĥes Mylys, de eadem, ac omnes, etc.

"Joĥes Mounford, de *Donn;* Ričus Godard, de Donn, husb.; Ričus Willyam, de Donn, husb.; Joĥes Petle, de Donn, husb.; Joĥes Smyth, de Donn, husb.; Wiĥs Mathewe, de Donn, husb.; Joĥes Erle, de Donn, yoman; Wiĥs Walleys, de Donn, gentilman; Joĥes Maynell, de *Codham;* et Joĥes Rowched, de Codham, ac omnes, etc.

"Joĥes Blowere, de *Rouchestre*, draper;[1] Robtus Bonham, de eadem, skryvener; Joĥes Fraunceys, de eadem, laborer; Nicĥus Picard, de eadem, smyth; Petrus Pierles, de eadem, bocher; Thomas Fuller, de eadem, bruer; Joĥes Blakburn, de eadem, bruer.

"Edmundus Chymbham, de parochia de *Southflete*, gent.; Wiĥs Edmond, de eadem, yoman; Ričus Jurdon, de eadem, yoman; Joĥes Shirwode, de eadem, yoman.

"Joĥes Frere, de *Strode*, shipman; Robtus Frere, de eadem, shipman; Robtus Worme, de eadem, barbour; Joĥes Cheseman, corveser; Thomas Hencote, de eadem, mason; Simon Hert, de eadem, shipman; Joĥes Hert, de eadem, shipman.

"Roǵus Appelton, senior, de *Derteford*, gentilman; Marǵia uẍ ejus, Roǵus Appelton, filius p̃dci Roǵi, de eadem, gent.; Thomas Herry, de eadem, yoman, ac omnes, etc.

"Thomas Undirdowne, de *Dertford*, watirman; Joĥes Underdowne, filius ipsius Thome, de eadem, watirman; et Joĥes Webbe, de eadem, watirman.

"Wiĥs Worthe, de Derteford, inholder; Walr̃us atte Heath,

[1] Membrane 6.

JOHN CADE'S FOLLOWERS IN KENT.

de eadem, ferrour; Ricus atte Heathe, filius ipsius Walti, de eadem, laborer; Ricus Holte, de eadem, sadler; Johes Page, de eadem, plomer; Johes Gubby, de eadem, chaundeler; Thomas Gubby, de eadem, laborer; Thomas Revet, de eadem, couper.

"Henr Ruste, *alias* Henr Rous, de *Crayford*, yoman; Stephus Large, de *Derteford*, yoman; Witts Herry, de eadem, barbour; Thomas Smyth, de eadem, yoman; Johes Baker, de eadem, inholder; Witts Fuller, de *Stone*, yoman; Rog'us Loundyssh, de *Southflete*, husbondman; Johes Turnour, de *Derteford*, couper.

"Stephus Rogger, de *Smerden*, bocher; Ricus Norton, de eadem; Johes Melle, husbondman; Witts Marlare, taillour, Thomas Elys, husb.; Laurencius Marlare, taillour; Nichus Engeherst, husb.; Johes Hogge, chapman; Johes Holstrete, husb.; Thomas Pell, husb.; Thomas Cook, husb.; Ricus Scott, clothmaker; Thomas Heyman, clothmaker; Robtus Heyman, clothmaker; Robtus Whithed, laborer; Olmerus Dowele, tyler; Johes Dowele, tyler; Johes Materas, bocher; Witts Materas, smyth; Witts Habynden, laborer; Thomas Stace, husbondman; Thomas Sharp, taillour; Witts Melle, senior, husb.; Robtus Tuysnoth, husb.; Thomas Tuysnoth, laborer; Johes Philpot, fletcher; Johes Blechynden, carpenter; Witts Blechynden, carpenter: Thomas Kene, de eadem, fuller; Henr Burwassh, carpenter; Ricus Romynden, bocher; Johes Hooke, corveser; Johes Clerk, baker; Thomas Clerk, corveser; Robtus Clerk, baker; Alcxus Sawyer, barbour; Johes Jaffrey, taillour; Johes Hamond, husb.; Witts Bromley, husb.; Witts Swyft, husb.; Thomas Fuller, sawyer; Henr atte Dene, husb.; Johes Colyn, thatcher; Johes Hunt, wever; Robtus Cheseman, laborer; Witts Philpot, colyer; Ricus Burncy, draper; Stephus Omynden, clothmaker; Robtus Dowenyng, turnour; Petrus Hoope, laborer; Ricus Blacche, laborer; Witts Hamond, sawyer; Johes Tobyll, laborer; Witts Tobyll, turnour; Laur Whytherynden, bocher; Johes Asshcombe, coryour; Johes Bocher, laborer; Ricus Bocher, carpenter; Witts atte Heye, laborer; Henr Cloke, laborer; Ricus Comber, laborer; Henr Baker, sawyer; Simon Melle, laborer; Henr Colyn, taillour; Phus

JOHN CADE'S FOLLOWERS IN KENT. 61

Baker, laborer; Ricus Baker, corveser; Stephus Baker, thatcher; Johes Glover, bocher; Ricus Glover, glover; Robtus Butterford, chapman; Wiłłs Engeherst, laborer; Robtus Couper, wever; Ricus Couper, laborer; Thomas Bresynden, fuller; Wiłłs Bresynden, thatcher; Laur Bresynden, sawyer; Henr Gervays, laborer; Johes Rede, laborer; Johes Tyernden, wever; Thomas atte Hoo, tanner; Johes atte Wode, husb.; Johes atte Wode, tanner; Wiłłs Hammc, smyth; Jacobus Bresynden, smyth; Johes Symond, laborer; Thomas Bailly, clothmaker; Wiłłs Bailly, wever; Thomas Bailly, wever; Johes Yve, wever; Wiłłs Newenden, laborer; Johes Cheseman, wever; Thomas Treton, turnour; Robtus Smyth, laborer; Henr Petyte, taillour; Johes Stone, laborer; Laur Pope, bocher; Ricus Bailly, wever; et Nichus Stykker, skynner.

"Thomas Burgeys, de *Gravene*, armig; et Johes Thornbury, de *Feversham*, armig.

"Thomas Ussher, de parochia *S'c'e Margarete juxta Roff*, husb.; Johes Hassok, de eadem, carpenter; Thomas Bradford, de eadem, husb.; et Thomas Brabon, de eadem, carpenter.

"Robtus Tuk, de parochia de *Esterfarlegh*, carpenter; Thomas Pestmyth, de eadem, mason; et Walus Prebyll, de eadem, husbondman.

"Edmundus Chertesey, de *Hedecrone*, gentilman; Thomas Burden, de parochia de Edecrone, husbondman; Thomas Baker, de eadem, draper; Michael Burden, de eadem, husbondman; Robtus Lytlesden, de eadem, husb.; Henr Brice, de eadem, bocher; et Thomas Edenden, de eadem, bocher.

"Johes Ferry, de *Gyllyngham*, yoman; Wiłłs Wynter, de *Pepybury*, husbondman; et Johes Floure, de eadem, husbondman.

"Ricus Cokset, de *Rouchestre*, yoman; Wiłłs Dunston, de eadem, yoman; Wiłłs Wyse, de eadem, yoman; Johes Rogger, de eadem, cordewayner; Ricus Yato, de eadem, yoman; Thomas Maunfeld, de eadem, taillour; et Johes Baker, de eadem, yoman.

"Johes Rede, de Rouchestre, senior, yoman; Johes Rede, de eadem, junior, yoman; Wiłłs Herry, de eadem, bruer; Laurencius Holbroke, de eadem, joynour; Nicħus Wever, de eadem, wever; et Robtus atte Wode, de *Asshe juxta Frenyngham*, yoman.

"Thomas Tebbe, de *Brynchesle*, yoman; et Thomas Brok, de *Marden*, yoman.

"Wiłłs Hereward, de *Rouchestre*, talloughchanndler; Wiłłs Wollys, de eadem, husb.; Joħes Malet, de eadem, chapman; Joħes Botswaync, de eadem, laborer; Joħes Couper, de eadem, s'uaunt; Robtus Omyllok, Wiłłs Godfrey, Nicħus Truley, Ričus Godfrey, Petrus Carpenter; et Wiłłs Coke.

"Wiłłs Estmere, Joħes Gybbe, Nicħus Sarles, Joħes Trukkys, Joħes Cok, Hen⁹ Polan, Joħes Heremyte, Wiłłs Wrothton, Henr̃ Waryn, Wiłłs Osbarn, Joħes Hamelet junior, Joħes Wadde, Joħes Hamelett senior, Joħes Bokenfold, Joħes atte Hecche, Wiłłs atte Wode, Thomas Pollard, Joħes May, Joħes Spuddell, Simon Canon, Wiłłs Crippys, Joħes Frende, Thomas Gillot, Joħes Symond, Joħes Colyn, Henr̃ Bedell, Ričus Poland, Wiłłs Grene, Thomas Robyn, Joħes Gilbe, Ričus Pollard, Wiłłs Pore, Thomas Upton, Wiłłs Wade, Simon Estlesse, Jacobus Gedewyn, Henr̃ John, Thomas Page, Joħes Slikdod, Joħes Ware, Hamandus Basset, Robtus Cokman, Wiłłs Grantham, Wiłłs Brodeville, Joħes Cosyn, Joħes Parys, Thomas Trill, Thomas Clerk, de parochia de *Upchirche*, husb.

"Joħes Dygges, de *Newyngton;* Ričus Dygges, de Newynton; Robtus Barford, de eadem; Thomas Herry, Joħes Herry, Joħes Thomas, Wiłłs Woddard, Joħes Clement, Wiłłs Geffray, Thomas Long, et Joħes Geffray, de villa et parochia de Newynton, in HUNDR' DE MILTON.

"Joħes Tredaunt, de *Asshford*, yoman; Joħes Wattes, de eadem, yoman; Wiłłs Egerynden, de eadem, bocher; et Petrus Kynet, de *Wyvelesbergh*, bocher.

"Joħes Ferry, de *Gyllyngham*, yoman; Wiłłs Wynter, de *Peppynbury*, husb.; et Joħes Floure, de eadem, husbondman.

"Wiłłs Brownyng, de *Herietisham*, yoman.

"David Wylkyn, de *Middelton*, shipman.

"Wiłłs Penyngton, de *Osprynge*, capellanus.

"Robtus Shayle, de *Maydeston;* et Ričus Wode, de eadem.

JOHN CADE'S FOLLOWERS IN KENT. 63

"Robtus Bettenham, de parochia de *Plukley*, gentilman; Radus Welde, de eadem, yoman; Wiłłs Gyles, de eadem, yoman; Ričus Tylgheman, de eadem, yoman; Henr̄ Hert, de eadem, yoman; Wiłłs Hoke, yoman; Ričus Dnoll, draper; Thomas Tylgheman, smyth; Ričus Pekenham, draper; Thomas Wanden, draper; Thomas Pix, carpenter; Wiłłs atte Forde, husb.; Stephus Piryfeld, couper; Ričus Child, carpenter; Valentinus Child, carpenter; Johes Godard, wever; Wiłłs Godard, wever; Johes Hert, husb.; Thomas Hert, husb.; Johes Best, husb.; Rogus Peteman, husb.; Rogus Bever, husb.; Wiłłs Monde, husbondman; Jacobus Bocher; Ričus Kyngessnoth, husb.; Wiłłs Kyngessnoth, husb.; Johes Brounsmyth, husb.; Johes Baker, tyler; Thomas Elys, husb.; Robtus Monde, husb.; Thomas Denys, husb.; Galfus Spyte, taillour; Wiłłs Materas, husb.; Johes Gybon, husb.; Thomas Philpot, husb.; Thomas Scot, husb.; Johes Rukke, laborer; Robtus Sawyere, laborer; Johes Sawyere, laborer; Johes Kyngessnoth, laborer; Johes Hassilherssh, laborer; Johes Hoget, laborer; Johes Bocher, fuller; Dionisius Rychard, taillour; Wiłłs Bocher, laborer; Wiłłs Doull, fuller; Thomas Kyngessnoth, fuller; Thomas Gybon, laborer; Georgius Baker, laborer; et Ričus Grenstrete, laborer, ac omnes, etc.

"Ričus Dyne, de *Maydeston*, gent.

"Johes Gouell, de *Boxle*, yoman; Henr̄ Asshby, yoman; Rogus Man, yoman; Robtus Man, yoman; Thomas Gulley, yoman; et Johes Clynton, de eadem, yoman.

"Johes Knyght, de *Charrying*, yoman.

"Thomas Heed, de *Plukle*, yoman, simul cum aliis.

"Johes Thrope, de *Ightham*, baker; Ričus Thrope, Johes Mercer, Wiłłs Godewyn, Wiłłs Sawyer, et Johes Smyth, de Ightham, ac omnes, etc.

"Johes Sencler, de *Feversham*, armig̃; Wiłł Barbour, de eadem, senior, gentilman; Simon Orwell, de eadem, bruer; Johes Ulf, de eadem, fysshmonger; Ričus Drayton, de eadem, bruer; Ričus Croft, de eadem, gentilman; Robtus Wastel, de eadem, bocher; Johes Orwell, de eadem, bruer; Johes London de eadem, yoman; Johes Poland, de eadem, glover; Wiłłs

Weeks, de eadem, bocher; Stephus White, de eadem, tanner; et Thomas Stede, de eadem, yoman.

"Rogus Heth, de *Ore*, husb.; Thomas Heth, nup de eadem villa, laborer; et Robtus Heth, de eadem villa, laborer.

"Wills Foughill, de Magna Chart, diere, CONSTABULARIUS HUNDR' DE CHART;[1] Johes Fogge, armig; Rogus Twysden, Wills Goldwell, Wills Assherst, husb.; Ricus Sprot, yoman; Johes Watte, yoman; et Johes Foughill, ac omnes, etc.

"Wills Egerynden, constabularius HUND' DE LONGEBRYGGE,[2] in parochia de Assheteford; Wills Brokman, de eadem, gent.; Johes Brokman, gent; Johes Werde, mercer; Alex Harry, sherman; Johes Tredaunt, tayllour; Marcus Salman, fletcher; et Ricus Burman, de eadem, chapman; ac omnes, etc.

"Johes Crips, de *Lenham*, yoman.

"Johes Salmon, Ricus Aleyn, Johes Roger, Thomas of Hoo, Wills Stevyn shipman, Johes Stephyn, Johes Carew, Johes Northwode, Johes Stephyn, de *Brokestrode;* Wills Whithayles, Johes Edward, Johes Balfyr, Hamudus Pere, Johes Baker, Ricus Baker, Thomas Baker, Henricus Northwode, Johes Wygyn, Thomas Porker, Henricus Baker, Henricus Colyn, Salmon Ryche, Gilbertus Bocher, Wills Stephyn, Johes Stephynson, Thomas Colyn, Johes Rose, Wills Whyttlalys senior, Johes Hopkyn, Ricus Copyn, Johes Craine, Henr Hamond, Henr Bochier, Wills Knepe, Thomas Rogers, Robtus Martyn, Adam Balsyre, Johes Porker, Ricus Shyhwassh, Henr Parker, Petrus Thomson, Wills Godfray, Johes Elmer, Wills Brodstrete, Ricus Brodstrete, Ricus Frensshe, Wills Osey, Thomas Osey, Thomas Martyn, Ricus Balfyr, Johes Dyrward, Robtus Carys, Johes Shepper, Wills Jonson, Johes Coole, Thomas Levyng, Thomas Janyn, Thomas Osey junior, Thomas Roger senior, Johes Boll, Johes Hopkyn, Thomas Pax, Johes Brade, Wills Balfyr, Thomas Boll, Henr Gylwyn, Johes Janyn, Thomas Derett, Johes Roger junior, Thomas Barbour, Johes Pax, Johes Strode, Johes Lunse, Wills Lunse, Johes Brede senior, Salmon Elmer, Thomas Elmer, Petrus Smyth, Robtus Brede, Johes Brede junior, Thomas Merssh, Johes Smelt,

---

[1] See *ante*, p. 41. [2] See *ante*, p. 41.

Johes Moys, Thomas Taillor, Thomas Brede, Wiłłs Coke, Cristoforus Boll, Johes Brede, Adam Edward, Wiłłs Aleyn, Johes German, Johes Taylor, Robtus Wellard, Wiłłs German, Wiłłs Shyppwassh, Wiłłs Olyf, Ričus Elnore, Johes Pottere, Johes Symond, ac omnes alii et singuli de parochia et HUND' DE WHYTSTAPLE.

"Wiłłs Wodegate, et Johes Wodegate, de *Edynbrygge*.

"Wiłłs Canon, de *Tenham*, maryner; et Ričus Reyson, de eadem, maryner.[1]

"Thomas Elys, of *Maydeston*, senior, husbondman; Thomas Elys, junior, husbondman; Johes Reder, husbondman; Thomas Master, husbondman; Thomas Luk, husbondman; Wiłłs Joce, husbondman; Thomas Peppymbury, de *Merden*, husbondman; Johes Harry, de *Lynton*, husbondman; Thomas Tylden, de *Merden*, husbondman; et Johes Stercough, de *Lynton*, husbondman; ac omnes, etc.

"Ričus Dene, de *Maydeston*, dobetchmaker; Alanus Gerard, smyth; Robtus Fordham, corvyser; Raďus Long, spyser; Johes Long, waxchaundeler; Ričus Long, barbour; Johes Crompe, barbour; Ričus Maynard, corvyser; Nichus Celkys, laborer; Johes Chapman; et Petrus Park, yoman; ac omnes, etc.

"Johes Hyllys, de *Horsmonden*, baker; Henr̃ Hykmot, et Ričus Bygland.

"Stephus Carder, de *Cranebroke*; et Thomas Carder, filius suus.

"Thomas Cotyng, de parochia de *Bakchyld*, yoman; Lodewico John, husb.; Thomas Messenger, husb.; Laurencius Danver, husb.; Ričus Bromfeld, husb.; Johes Messenger, senior, husb.; Johes Messenger, junior, husb.; Adam Messenger, husb.; Nichus Newenton, husb.; Robt Crewese, husb.; Roǧus Stampyke, husb.; Nichus Cloue, husb.; Johes Wayman, husb.; Wiłłs Wayman, husb.; Robtus Wylson, husb.; Johes Metar, husb.; Benedc̃s Metar, husb.; Wiłłs Russell, husb.; Wiłłs Steker, husb.; Henr̃ atte Wode, husb.; et Stephus Peere, husbondman, ac omnes, etc.

"Ričus Smyth, de *Shorne*; Johes Smyth, Wiłłs Hamme, Johes Davy, Johes Hauke, Petrus Hauke, Petrus Page, Thomas Bedill, Ričus Yong, Thomas Coke, et Ričus Neweman.

[1] Membrane 5.

"Adam Dane, de *Bredherst*, husbondman; Roḡus Rolff, husb.; Witts Gildewyne, husb.; Joñes Kemmysle, husb.; Joñes Fylle, husb.; Thomas Sayyere, husb.; Thomas Costedyll, de eadem, husb.; Thomas Flete, de *Boxle*, husb.; Joñes Stretys, senior, husb.; Thomas Stretys, junior, de eadem, yoman; Joñes Jelyffe, de *Gelyngham*, husb.; Witts Bratyll, husb.; Joñes Well, de eadem, laborer; Adam Stretys, de *Bredhurst*, husb.; et Petrus Page, de *Stokebury*, laborer.

"Bernardus Kawyll, de *Chesylherst*, CONSTABULAR' HUNDR' DE ROKYSLEY; Pħus atte Well, de *Orpyngton*; Witts Miller, de Orpyngton; Thomas Stabyll, de *Cray b'e Marie*; Joñes Petely, de *Downe*; Joñes Jeter, de *Chelseld*; Roƀtus Mabelote, de *Orpyngton*; Vinsensius Broke de Orpyngton; et Ričus Wallsshe, de *Cray b'e Marie*.

"Joñes Gate, de *Estgrenwiche*, bocher, et Marḡia ux ejus; Ricus Henham, carpenter, et Marḡia ux ejus; Ričus Gate, reder, et Margareta ux ejus; Ričus Fox, laborer, et Petronilla ux ejus; Joñes Berde, couper, et Margareta ux ejus; Simon Nele, pulter, et Petronilla ux ejus; Nicħus Astyng, taillour, et Marḡia ux ejus; Raďus Denys, baker, et Alicia ux ejus; Joñes Lavender, de eadem, bocher; et Roƀtus Herny, de eadem, barbour.

"Thomas Elbrigge, de *Rouchestre*, tauerner, et Johanna ux ejus; Witts Thurston, yoman; Thomas Maunsell, taillour; et Ričus Nicoll, de eadem, tynker, ac omnes, etc.

"Hugo Godewyn, gent; et Ričus Culpeper, gent; ac omnes, etc.

"Joñes Payne, de parochia de *Merworth*, gentilman; Roƀtus Chamberleyn, de eadem, gentilman; et Joñes Taillour, de eadem, husb.; ac omnes, etc.

"Thomas Sport, de *Middelton*, smyth; Henr̄ Malls, shipman; Witts Maas, shipman; Ričus Shipman, husb.; Witts Cok, shipman; Joñes Tresbon, husb.; Joñes Bragh, fuller; Alanus Baron, cordwayner; Witts Role, tanner; Sampson atte Style, barbour; Thomas Sane, shipman; Joñes Stepemham, shipman; Gerardus Rus, bereman; Thomas Stevyn, shipman; Joñes Cok, shipman; Henr̄ Wythlok, shipman; Joñes Symnet, shipman, Wiłts Symnet, shipman; Wiłts Symmet, shipman; Nichus Gate, roper; Johes Noke, bocher; Wiłts Bugge, husbondman: Johes Bugge, husbondman; et Thomas Echet, husbondman.

"Wiłts Grene, et Thomasia ux ejus.

"Laurencius Levyngdall.

"Thomas atte Wode, de parochia de *Holyngborn*, in HUND' DE HEYBORN, husbondman; ac omnes, etc.

"Jacobus Cheynwe, de *Westeram*, gent.

"Johes Aston, de *Maydeston*, yoman; et Barthus Guerdon; et Ricus Aston, de *Gowteherst*, yoman.

"Johes Rychefeld, Thomas Tyrry, constabularius HUNDR' DE RYNGYSLOWE; Wiłts Manston, Thomas Saynt Nichus, Johes Sandeway; et Johes Malyn.

"Ricus Chalkhill, de *Maydeston*.

"Thomas Godyng, de *Yeldyng*, yoman; et Johes Snode, *Hunton*, husb.

"Johes Clyfford, de *Bobbyng*, armig; et Wiłts Norton, de *Sheldwych*, armig.

"Wiłts Downe, de *Westmallyng*, gent.; Robtus Langley, de parochia de Westmallyng, gent.; et Wiłts Gunne, de eadem, yoman.

"Wiłts Robert, de parochia de *Hese*, husb.;[1] Johes Heuer, husb.; Ricus Shot, husb.; Ricus Aleyn, husb.; Alanus Nassh, husb.; Johes Aleyn, husb.; Hugo Kechill, husb.; Wiłts Frensshe, husb.; et Simon Kechill, husb.; ac omnes, etc.

"Richus Nether, de hund. de *Beknam et Bromeley*, yoman; Robtus Payn, de eadem, yoman; Henr̄ Payn, yoman; et Thomas Thornton, de eadem, yoman.

"Hugo atte Wode, of *Ealdyng*, gentilman; Johes Orger, yoman; Wiłts Water, yoman; et Ricus Coueney, chapman; constabularii de HUNDR' de TWYFORD.

"Johes Elphy, de parochia de *Burlyng*, carpenter; Ricus Welcok, de eadem, carpenter; et Wiłts Broune, de eadem, carpenter.

"Ricus Bolt, de *Denton*, husb.; Johes Bolt, husb.; Ricus

[1] Membrane 4.

Vcisy, husb.; Ričus Osbern, husb.; Joħes Bisshop, de eadem, husb.; Andreas Wilby, de *Chalk*, husb.; Thomas Kebbyll, nuper de *Shorne*, grome; et Joħes Kebbyll, grome.

"Thomas Huchon, Joħes Godfrey senior, Joħes Godfrey junior, Joħes Aleyn, Ričus atte Crowche; Roḃtus Prall, Thomas Dyne, Nicħus Bosyne, Roḃtus Rolf, Clemens Rolf, Thomas atte Strete, Roḃtus Godfrey, Roǧus Murstok, Roḃtus Halstok; et Wiħs Poynant, de parochia de *Stone*, in hunđ de Oxney, husbondmen; Henr̃ Northland, Wiħs Moseden; et Wiħs Kynet, de parochia de *Ebney*, in eadem hunđ, husbondmen.

"Ričus Toly, vynter; et Joħes Grene, yoman.

"Hugo Caxton, de *Sandewico*, mercer; Ričus Halk, de eadem, chapman; Wiħs Nede, de eadem, spycer; Thomas Davy, de eadem, barbour; Thomas Bromer, de eadem, chapman; Henr̃ Chadilwode, de eadem, chapman; Joħes Pette, de eadem, bruer; et Nicħus Saunder, de eadem, taloughchaundler.

"Ričus Joskyn, de *Cobham*, senior, husb.; Joħes Joskyn, de eadem, yoman; Joħes Sprever, de eadem, bocher; Wiħs Sprever, de eadem, senior, yoman; Wiħs Sprever, de eadem, junior, yoman; Walt̃us Shippe, de eadem, yoman; Henr̃ Stace, de eadem, husb.; Thomas Wright, de eadem, yoman; et Walt̃us Stace, de eadem, senior, yoman; ac omnes, etc.

"Thomas Kelsham, gent.; Ričus Burden, Michael Burden, Thomas Burden, Petrus Widynbroke, Thomas Baker, Thomas Homersham, Thomas Widynbroke, Thomas Edynden, Simon Whitsperok, Henricus atte Well, Joħes Hamersham, Walt̃us Turnour, Ričus Hasper, Thomas Turnour, Joħes Frary, Joħes Fuller, Joħes Bowdon junior, Thomas Thornherst, Henr̃ Hamond, Thomas Fuller, Roḃtus Lellisden, Petrus Hoigge senior, Wiħs Grigge, Joħes Fox, Wiħs Manne, Stepħus Manne, Simon Hoigge, Rađus Blechynden, Thomas Blechynden, Roǧus Bakere, Rađus Bayman, Joħes Gateman junior, Rađus Blechynden, Stepħus Rede, Joħes Bachelere, Roǧus Turnour, Joħes Turnour, Wiħs Sandir, Wiħs Hamme, Roǧus Edynden, Galfr̃us atte Wode, Rađus Baily, Joħes atte Crowche, Thomas Baily, Rađus atte Crowche, Roḃtus Burghaissh, Ričus at Chambir, Joħes Thornherst, Thomas Prat, Stepħus Symme, Joħes Ropere, Heñ

JOHN CADE'S FOLLOWERS IN KENT. 69

Burden, Thomas Birchet, Johes Hovynden, Petrus atte Brigge, Johes atte Brigge junior, Johes Bishop, Henr̃ Bisshop, Wiħs Bysshop, Petrus Hoigge junior, Stepħus Boycote, Stepħus Adam, Thomas Bakere, Joħes atte Tonge, Roǧus Hamond, Roƀtus Marketman, Joħes Burdon, Joħes Southlond, Joħes Grigge, Henr̃ Grigge, Stepħus Elcok, Henr̃ Brice, Joħes Boicote, Joħes Gateman senior, Thomas Boicote, Roƀtus Whithede, Wiħs Gune, Joħes Swyneham, Joħes Whitsperehauke, Henr̃ Whitsperehauke, Thomas Pix, Joħes Blachynden, Walƿus Gaunt, de parochia de *Hedecorn*.

"Walƿus Brencheley, de parochia de *Denynden*, gent.; Joħes Sharp, de eadem, yoman; Joħes Wylert, de eadem, yoman; Roƀtus Wolf, de eadem, yoman; Thomas Stays, de eadem, yoman; Wiħs Keppyng, de eadem, yoman.

"Wiħs Sandhirste, de *Lamberhirste*, yoman; et Joħes Martyn, de *Brynchesle*, yoman.

"Ričus Coise, de *Spelhurst*, yoman; et Wiħs Knyght, de *Pepynbury*, yoman.

"Thomas Carter, de *Maideston*, draper; Wiħs Brok, barbour; Wiħs Smyth, mason; Thomas Clavering, grocer; Ričus Carter, draper; Wiħs Colyn, wexchaundler; Hamo Clerk, barbour; Joħes Brok, de *Ealdyng*, wever; Ričus Piers, de eadem, draper; et Ričus Maunfeld, de eadem, barbour.

"Joħes Baker, de *Horsmonden*, husb.; Stepħus Baker, coteler; Ričus Baker, glover; Laurencius Baker, laborer; Wiħs Olyver, sƿuant; Ričus Joce, husb.; Wiħs Cloute, carpenter; Stepħus Cloute, carpenter; et Jacobus Hulles, husb.; ac omnes, etc.

"Thomas Harry, et Joħes Rychevile, constabularij HUND' DE RYNGSLOUE; ac Wiħs Manston, et Joħes Septvans, ac omnes, etc.[1]

"Joħes Prat, de *Maideston*, carpenter; Thomas Dousynd, husb.; Thomas Swyft, smith; Ričus Plotte, carpenter; Thomas Russell, yoman; Joħes Clobyer, cornester; Wiħs Humfrey, smyth; Thomas Lott, laborer; Roƀtus Fyssher, taillour; et Ričus Deanden, de eadem, laborer.

[1] See *ante*, p. 67.

"Johes Cokeram, MAIOR VILLE N'RE DE QUENEBURGH, marchaunt;[1] Johes Swalman, de Queneburgh, yoman; Wiłłs Baker, baker; Wiłłs Britte, maryner; Johes Britte, maryner; Johes Masyn, maryner; Wiłłs Canon, maryner; Alanus Jacob, maryner; Galfrus Benet, maryner; Robtus Somter, maryner; et Johes Willys, de Queneburgh, maryner.

"Ričus Smyth, de *Westram*, yoman; Thomas Stacey, taner; Johes Man, husb.; Wiłłs Chawry, husb.; et Thomas Gillot, husb., de eadem.

"Johes Cok, et Thomas Pycard, constabularij hund de LITLE et LESYN; ac omnes, etc.[2]

"Ričus Berbet, de *Hastynglye*, husbondman; Wiłłs Serles senior, husb.; Thomas Serles, husb; Stephus Mathewe, husb., de eadem; Wiłłs Serles, de *Wy*, husb.; et Thomas Bette, de eadem, husb.

"Henr̄ Pakeman, de *Hoo*, husb.; Johes Never, husb.; et Johes Malyt, de eadem, husb.

"Johes Clerke, psona ecclie de *Halgesto*,[3] in hund de Hoo; Simon Dalam, husb.; et Johes Neweman, de eadem, husb."

The repetition of names in several distinct pardons may show that the lists were hurriedly sent in: but, as the constables of some of the hundreds are twice entered on the roll, and in some instances the names differ, it may be that the pardons are for the separate risings: the one for the original advance to Blackheath, and the other for the second and more formidable advance after the affray at Sevenoaks.

[1] The charter was granted in 1366. [2] See *ante*, p. 53.
[3] See *ante*, p. 47.

JOHN CADE'S FOLLOWERS IN SUSSEX.[1]

BY WILLIAM DURRANT COOPER, F.S.A., &c.

THE part taken by Sussex men in the rising has been very slightly noticed by our historians. The chroniclers vary in their descriptions of Cade's followers: Holinshed says, as we have seen, that he drew to him from Kent " a great company of tall personages;"[2] but he calls the others "divers idle and vagrant persons out of the shire, Sussex, Surrie, and other places."[2]

So far as Sussex, and especially East Sussex, was concerned, the rising partook, like Kent, very much of the character of a military and duly authorised levy and array. In many hundreds the musters were levied by the constables; the small landowners (the yeomen), with their labourers, and some tradesmen, were ready in their appearance, and we have by name upwards of 400 Sussex men present.

The state of Sussex was such that it might well cause discontent. The Bishop (Adam Moleyns, who was murdered on the 9th January, 1450,) had been prominent among the King's very unpopular councillors; the French had landed with impunity, doing considerable damage; and many complaints were current of the mode in which the fifteenths were collected.[3] Lord Say and Sele (James Fiennes), the Lord Treasurer, was unfavourably known in Sussex as having just acquired his title by grant, from John de Clinton, his Sussex kinsman; and it will be seen

---

[1] The substance of this portion was also printed in vol. xviii. of the Sussex Archæological Collections.

[2] The Essex and Suffolk men joined only when Cade was in the city.

[3] The House of Commons had previously called the attention of the Government to the murders, rapes, robberies, and burnings that pervaded this county. *Rot. Parl.* (1430), p. 421,

that the neighbours of de Clinton at Hamsey, and the men living close by the Treasurer's eldest brother, Sir Roger Fiennes (who had built Herstmonceux Castle), and Thomas Dacre, of Bailey Park, Heathfield, in whose service John Cade had been, turned out the strongest in the lists of Cade's Sussex followers.

The Abbot of Battle (Richard Dertmouth), and the newly-chosen Prior of Lewes (John Danyel), with their respective communities,[1] sanctioned the movement, and were involved in the consequences; and their example was followed by the Bailiffs of Pevensey and Seaford, and the Constables of the Borough of Lewes, with the Burgesses of the same town.

There joined him out of Sussex the Apsleys, Barttelots, Bartholomew Bolney, who had some ten years before acquired the manor of West Firle,[2] the Burtons, Chaloners, Colbronds, Gilderidges, Laddes, Lunsfords, Melewards, Oxenbridges, Parkers, Robert Poynings, of Twincham and Sutton, who is described as having stirred the great part of such as were adherents, and accompanied Cade and was his carver and sword-bearer,[3] the Selwins, Wolffes, and many others, who subsequently held office under or warmly supported Edward IV.

The immediate provocation given to Kent by the harshness with which the men of that county were threatened in consequence of the killing of the Duke of Suffolk, and by the oppressions alleged against William Crowmer, then Sheriff, and Lord Say's son-in-law, did not apply to Sussex, and this county did not join till after the second advance towards London at the commencement of July.[4]

Before noon on the Thursday, the day the Staffords were killed at Sevenoaks,[5] the King and 20,000 armed men entered

[1] So also did Katherine De la Pole, the Abbess of St. Mary, Barking, Essex. Mem. 9.
[2] He lies buried at West Firle; his daughter Agnes, in 1472, married Wm. Gage, and carried the Firle estate into that family. There is a brass to him and his wife; and there is a brass in Fletching church for J. Reynolds, *post*, p. 77.
[3] *Rot. Parl.* v. p. 396.
[4] Cade's head-quarters were at the White Horse in Southwark.
[5] Holinshed says that Cade " apparelled himself in Sir Humphrey's brigandine, set full of guilt nailes, and so in some glorie returned again toward London."

the camp at Blackheath. The Lord Say and William Crowmer were arrested and committed to the Tower.

Cade and his followers entered London. Wm. Wyrcester says a commission of Oyez and Terminer was then made, and Robert Danvers was made Justiciary.[1] And the Duke and Duchess of Suffolk, the Bishop of Salisbury [i.e. Askewe, already dead], the Lord de Saye, Thomas Danyell, John Saye, and many others, were indicted of treason in the Guildhall of London; and after this, on the 4th July next following, James Fynys Lord de Saye, in the 7th hour in the afternoon, was beheaded at the Standard in Chepe, and on the same day Wm. Crowmer, theretofore Sheriff of Kent, was beheaded by the said Captain without Aldgate, and a certain Thomas Bayly, Necromancer, or Diviner (nigromanticus vel geomanticus), at the White Chapel beyond the said Aldgate, was beheaded on the same day by the said Captain of Kent, which said Thomas had formerly been of the same way of thinking (cogitatione) with the same captain and of the like art[2] (et una arte); and on the Sunday following [5th July] William Hawerdene, a chief counsellor of the captain and a common thief, was hung by the Captain's order at Smithfield; and on the same night the Citizens, out of fear of the robbery of their goods, after a lengthened fight on London Bridge against the Captain and his people (gentes) of Kent, drove them into Southwark;[3] many however were killed on both sides, and amongst others there was unfortunately slain Matthew Gouche, an old captain and very noted in the King's wars.[4] And in like manner was there slain John Sutton, then an Alderman of the city.[5]

---

[1] He had been elected Recorder 14th July, 1442, and on 14th Aug. of the year 1450 he was made a Judge of the Common Pleas by Henry IV., so that his conduct as Justiciary had pleased the King's Commissioners.   [2] Took art and part.

[3] At 9 a.m. the Londoners, says Holinshed, had been driven back to St. Magnus church.

[4] He had been a distinguished soldier in France.

[5] The late Mr. G. R. Corner, F.S.A., in the *Surrey Arch. Coll.*, vol. ii. p. 66, following many histories, has erroneously dated the battle of the Bridge as 8th July. See the *Paston Letters*, vol. i. p. 57, for an amusing account by Payne, a servant of Sir John Falstolf, who had been taken by the rebels, and was present for six hours at this " battle of the Bridge."

74   JOHN CADE'S FOLLOWERS IN SUSSEX.

On the morrow of the 6th July, (after the Bishop of Winchester (William Waynflete) and others of the King's Council had held conference with the said Captain of Kent in the church of St. Margaret of Southwark,[1] and there received the bills of petitions; and in like manner had considered of a charter of pardon) the Captain and his commons retired to Rochester; and after this Alexander Iden was made Sheriff.

It is more probable, that, instead of the Chancellor[2] (John Kempe, Cardinal Archbishop of York), and the Bishop of Winchester (Waynflete) passing from the Tower, "bringing with them under the King's Great Seal a general pardon unto all the offenders," and causing the same to be openly published, and the poor men being "so glad of this pardon that without bidding farewell to their Captain they withdrew themselves the same night," Kempe, who was a man of Kent, and had for a short time held the see of Chichester, and whose mother was a Sussex Lady (Lewknor),[3] and Bishop Waynflete (his brother John was afterwards Dean of Chichester), were most anxious to restore peace and to induce Cade and his followers, many of whom must have been personally well known to the Cardinal, to accept pardons.

Cade's own pardon recites that a certain John Mortimer, together with several others, in no small but to a large and great number, in many and divers places within the realm, and especially in the county of Kent and places adjoining and convenient, without the King's mandate or authority, but of their own accord, lately assembled themselves and were led against the King contrary to law, &c., and then the pardon is to the said John and all others who had so associated and congregated.

The next entry on the roll is of pardons, not dated, for Wm. Tyrell, jr. esq., Matthew Hay, esq., John Batell, esq., Richard

[1] At the dissolution of monasteries St. Margaret's and St. Mary's were united into St. Saviour's.
[2] Kempe, and not the Archbishop of Canterbury, was then Chancellor.
[3] The Lewknors remained staunch in their loyalty to Henry. The Cardinal's maternal grandmother was the heiress of the Dalingrudges; and so he was not "unconnected with any noble or influential family." Besides, the brother of his paternal grandfather had married a Neville of Raby.

Shodewell, gentilman, Roger Wyke, of Colchester, and Richard Stace, sen., for treason at several places in Essex, Middlesex, and London; then, dated the same 6th July, are pardons for the three citizens of Canterbury.

On the following day pardons for the other followers by name were sealed; and whereas Cade's was directed to "all Bailiffs," these were directed to the respective counties of Kent, Sussex, Surrey, Essex, and Suffolk.

There is the name of one person of Devonshire, and one of the city of Oxford; one also, John Hereford, is described as an Irishman; he is called late of Kilkenny, yoman, but is in the same pardon with two other Herefords, one of London and the other of Bristol, so he was doubtless an Englishman, and the Irishmen were not involved in this rising, though the Duke of York was then in that country, and in the King's proclamation Cade is said to have been "born in Ireland."

The list of the Sussex men whose names are set out in the pardons is as follows,[1] and it is only necessary to note the grades of those who were involved. The esquires, of whom Kent furnished 18, are absent in Sussex; there are however several gentlemen and yeomen whose families are among our present landowners; the chaplain of Mayfield and the clerks of Dallington and Wartling are also there. The husbandmen are distinguished from the labourers.

Thomas Pyke de *Notehurst*,[2]	yoman.	Thomas Polyngton, de *Notehurst*, yoman.		
John Elby, of	,,	yoman.		
William Lucas	,,	husbondman.	John Croft ,, parker, and others.	
John Bottyng	,,	husbondman.		
Stephen Bottyng	,,	husbondman.	John Foreby, of *Idfeld*, gent.	
John Monke	,,	laborer.	Thomas Attewell, of *Bukstede*, gent.	
William Benke	,,	laborer.	William Bailly, of *Maghfeld*, gent.	
John Selede	,,	laborer.	Thomas Baker, of *Ukfeld* yoman.	
Thomas Weller	,,	tayllour.	William Manser, of ,, yoman, and	

---

[1] In these Sussex pardons I have given the Christian names in English and the whole in columns.

[2] Membrane 13.

William Pont, of *Magfeld*, yoman, constables of the HUNDRED OF LOKESFELD, and all and other men resident within the said Hundred.

Thomas Buste, of *Ryngmore*, yoman, and Andrew Thaccher, of „ yoman; constables of the HUNDRED of RINGMERE, and the residents of that HUNDRED.

Thomas Gymmour, of *Westfyrle*, gentilman, and

John Bysshe, of the same, yoman; together with others.

Gabriel Berword, of *Tysherst*, yoman, and

John Holbeme, of the same, yoman, constables of the HUNDRED of SHOESWELL.

Richard Fynche, of *Heighton*, husbondman,[1] and

William Herston, of *Bishopstone*, husbondman, constables of the HUNDRED of FLEXBERGH, and

Richard Dunton, of *Bisshopestone*, husbondman.

William Gofferay, of *Blachyngton*, husbondman.

Richard Clerk, of *Heighton*, husbondman.

Richard atte Lay, of *Denton*, husbondman.

Richard Chyntyng, of *Petynghoo*, husbondman, and

John Walkelyn, of *Meehyng*, senior, yoman, constables of the HUNDRED of HOLMSTROWE.

John Shulder, of *Radmylde*, husbondman.

John Theccher, of *Southese*, husbondman.

John Allecok, of *Tetelescombe*, husbondman.

John Porter of *Petynghoo*, laborer, and others of the Hundred aforesaid.

John Grene, of *Sheple*, gentylman
Richard Weller, of same, husbondman
John Waller „ husbondman.
Richard Attelowe „ husbondman.
Roger Fourlonger „ husbondman.
John Fourlonger „ husbondman.
Robert Offyngton „ husbondman.
William Folvyle „ husbondman.
Thomas Edwyn „ husbondman.
Roger Joppe „ laborer.
William Atte Herst „ laborer.
Roger Mayster „ laborer.
Richard Wyker „ laborer.
Roger Streter „ laborer.
John Valyor „ laborer.
John Mychell „ laborer.
John Creps „ laborer.
Richard Pacche „ laborer.

John Dowte, of *West grenstede*, husbondman.

Ralph Parson, of *Stenynge*, husbondman.

John Apsley, of same, junior.
John Broker „ husbondman.
John Maunsell „ husbondman.
Robert Hunt „ laborer.
Richard Frensshe „ laborer.
Stephen Champeneys „ husbondman.
John Colman „ laborer.

Roger Wolffe, of *Assyngton*, gentilman.
John Wolffe, of same, gentilman.
William Bouchy „ husbondman.
John Cradyll „ laborer.
William Chapman „ carpenter.
John Waterman „ laborer.
Laurence Perys „ laborer.

Richard Pollard, of *Wassington*, husbondman.
Thomas Webhe, of same, laborer.
John Hardyng „ laborer.
Lawrence Couper „ couper.
John Long „ junior.
Clement Cayn

[1] Mem. 12.

JOHN CADE'S FOLLOWERS IN SUSSEX.

William Capelayn, of same, husbandman.
Robert Capelayn „ husbandman.
James Pacchyng „ carpenter.

Thomas atte Hille, of *Wormynherst*, husbondman.
Richard Parker, of W., webbe.
Thomas Waterman „ husbondman.
William Heryssh „ laborer.
James Turgys „ laborer.
Richard Melward „ laborer.
John Bregger „ junior, with many others.

Henry Lecheford, of *Cranveley*, gentilman.

John Mabsyn, of *Cattysfeld*,[1] and
John Parker, of *Hoo*, constables of the HUNDRED of NENFELD; and
Henry Mabsyn, of *Cattysfeld*, with others.

Richard Beche, of *Setelescombe*, yoman, and
Robert Mortfote, of *Ewherst*, draper, constables of the HUNDRED of STAPLE, and others.

Thomas Andrewe, of *Laughton*, yoman. and
Richard Melewerd, of *Chidynglegh*, yoman, constables of the HUNDRED of SHEPLAKE, and
Henry atte Bregge, of *Laughton*, junior, yoman.
Thomas Upton „ yoman.
Richard Edewyn „ yoman.
John atte Legh „ yoman.
Thomas Frytour „
William Snoddon „ yoman and
William Lulham, of *Rype*, yoman, and others.

John Reynold, of *Fleethyng*, yoman.

Peter Dynot, of *Fleethyng*, glover.
Thomas White „ husbondman.
William Strode „ yoman.
Richard Lye „ pedeler.
Nicholas Cowper „ bocher, and others.

Robert Pepisden, of *Salchurst*, husbondman, and
Robert Braban, of same, husbondman, constables of the HUNDRED of HENHURST, &c.

Thomas Fynhawe, of *Westifeld*, and
Cristofer Halle, of *Crowhurst*, constables of the HUNDRED of BALDESLOWE, &c.

Richard Oxenbregge, of *Posemersh*, constable of the HUNDRED of COLSPORE, &c.
William Howlette, of *Brede*, husbondman, and
William Hunte, of *Odemere*, husbondman, constables of the HUNDRED of GODSTOWE, &c.

Robert atte Mille, of *Wartlyng*, yoman, and
Robert atte Wode, of *Warbylton*, husbondman, constables of the HUNDRED of FOXHEBLE, &c.

John Chaloner, of *Lynfeld*, yoman, and
Roger Russell, „ yoman, and others.
John Cook, of *Lewes*, and
John Bekquyth, of the same, constables of the town or BOROUGH of LEWES, and the burgesses of the same town.

Wm. Hokeby, of *Aylesham*, and
Richard Heggyngworth, of *Walderne*, constables of the HUNDRED THILLE, and
Thomas Wonnemer, of *Aylesham*.
Richard Turner „

[1] M. 11.

JOHN CADE'S FOLLOWERS IN SUSSEX.

Stephen Maynard, of *Aylesham*.
John Sander „ and others.
Robert Dereham, of *Horeham*, yoman, &c.
William Fysher, of *Wadeherst*, carpenter.
Gilbert Skynner, of same, husbondman.
John Bury „ draper.
John Crotehole „ husbondman.
Thomas Kyngewode „ tanner.
John Cobbe, of *Perpoundeshirst*, yoman.
Thomas Henfeld „ yoman.
Richard Atte wode „ yoman, and others.

William West,
Richard Allyn,
John Yam, and
Robert Abram, of *Robertsbrygge*, and the dwellers in that TOWN.

Thomas Waller, of *Fokyngton*,[1] yoman.
John Drewe, of *Jeuyngton*, yoman, and Thomas Hendyman, of *Wannok* or *Fokington*, yoman.
Thomas Drewe, of *Otham*, yoman.
Walter Reynold, of *Fokyngton*, husbondman.
John Fotonr, of *Wotton*, husbondman.
Roger Fotonr, of *Wannok*, yoman.
John Eyr, of *Fokyngton*, yoman.
Robert Frenssh „ yoman.
William Reynold „ husbondman.
Geffry Russell „ yoman.
Geffry Russell „ husbondman.
Geffry Hendyman, of *Wannok*, husbondman.
William Renne, of *Jeuyngton*, husbondman.
Laurence Renne „ husbondman.
Thomas atte Welle, of *Fokyngton*, husbondman.
Henry Raynold „ husbondman.
Thomas Phylpot „ husbondman and others.

[1] M. 10.

Richard Holforde, of *Flecchyng*, husbondman, constable of the HUNDRED of DENHILLE.
William Hode, of F., bocher.
Thomas Akecok „ carpenter, and
Philip Cabell „ husbondman, together with others of the hundred aforesaid.

John [Danyel], Prior of the Priory of SAINT PANCRAS OF LEWES, in the county of Sussex, and the convent of the same place, and all the men and servants of the same Priory or Convent.

Thomas Stevene, of *Dalyngton*,[2] yoman.
John Hogge „ laborer.
John Lambe „ yoman.
Thomas Hunte „ yoman.
William Tayllour „ clerk.
Adam Wodsil „ yoman.
William Sterlyng „ laborer.
Stephen Alfryge „ laborer.
Simon Rook, „ yoman.
Simon Croucher. „ laborer, and all and singular of the same TOWN.

Thomas de Dene, of *Dalyngton*, yoman.
John Martyn „ laborer.
Richard Cok „ laborer.
Laurence Cok „ laborer.
Thomas Polyngworde „ laborer.
Thomas Russell „ yoman.
Simon Russell „ laborer.
John Prior „ laborer, and all and singular of the same PARISH.

Simon Batys, of *Britlyng*, gentilman.
John Erle „ laborer.
John Martyn „ laborer.
Thomas Twyford „ laborer.
Nicholas Jolyf „ laborer.
William Meryfeld „ yoman.

[2] M. 9.

JOHN CADE'S FOLLOWERS IN SUSSEX. 79

John Meryfeld, of *Britlyng*, yoman.
John Bele „ laborer.
John Pouke „ laborer, and all and singular of the same TOWN.

William Burford, of *Britlyng*, yoman, and
Richard Wyker, of *Bataill*, yoman, constables of the HUNDRED of NETERFELD.

John Snayleham, of *Britlyng*, laborer.
Thomas Hert „ laborer.
Richard Bayly „ laborer.
John Wodeman „ laborer.
Thomas Godesole „ yoman.
Stephen Crotehole „ laborer.
Walter Martyn „ laborer.
William Smalefeld „ laborer.
John Kenne „ laborer.
William Haylok „ laborer.
John Adam „ laborer.
John Godehyne „ laborer,
and all and singular of the same HUNDRED.

Stephen Wyt, of *Mundefeld*, senior, yoman.
Stephen Wyt „ junior, yoman.
William Westbourne „ laborer.
John Norman „ laborer.
Richard atte Wode „ yoman.
John Kempe „ laborer.
William Cropwode „ yoman.
William Crecy „ laborer.
John Cropwode „ yoman.
Thomas Smyth „ yoman.
John Smyth „ yoman.
Richard Riche „ laborer.
John Horsman „ laborer.
John Hukstepe „ yoman.
John Hukstepe „ junior, laborer.
Robert Loke „ yoman,
and all and singular of the same PARISH.

John Forger, of the Parish of *All Saints, Lewes*, and all and singular of the same PARISH.

John Wryther, of the *Cliff juxta Lewes*, marchant.
John Chamberlayn „ yoman.
John Lardener „ yoman.
Thos. Podey, senior, „ yoman.
Andrew Somer „ glover.
William Cheseman „ yoman.
Richard Cole „ chapman.
William Bourehunte „ smyth.
Richard Benet „ sherman.
Thomas Cheseman „ chapman.
John Worth, „ yoman,
and all and singular of the TOWNSHIP aforesaid.

Bartholomew Bolney, of *Westfyrle*, gentilman, and all the men and servants of the said Bartholomew Bolney.

William Hampton, *Balliff of Pevensee*, yoman.
John Morley, of *Westham*, gentilman.
Richard Porter „ yoman.
Richard Motard „ yoman,
and all and singular the men dwelling in the TOWNS aforesaid.

Richard Selewyn, of *Selmyston*, gentilman.

William Colyn, and John Potman, constables of the HUNDRED of TOTNORE.

Richard Ballard, of *Westfyrle*, and Thomas Eton, of the same, and all and singular of the same HUNDRED.

John Hereward of *Erlyngton*, gentilman.
William Grent, „ senior, yoman.
Richard Delve, of *Michelham*, yoman.
Richard Fotur of, *Wylmyngton*, yoman.
Richard de Milton, of *Milton*, senior yoman.
Richard Roper, of *Lollington*, husbondman.
John Wyngeton, of *Erlyngton*, tailor.

JOHN CADE'S FOLLOWERS IN SUSSEX.

John Warrener, of *Milton*, laborer.
Robert Smyth, of *Wyngeton*, husbondman.
Thomas Smyth „ husbondman.
John Lencote, of *Alfriston*, laborer.
Simon Lencote „ laborer, and all and singular the men of the same TOWN.

Thomas Busty, of *Haylesham*,[1] gentilman.
John Sherman, of same, corveser.
Robert Bystrete ,, tanner.
Thomas Dobbys „ tailor.
Michael Haryot „ corveser.
John Knyght „ laborer.
Andrew Page „ yoman.
John Grent „ tanner.
Robert Gilderygge „ yoman.
William Osbern „ butcher.
Walter Osbern ,, yoman.
John Osbern „ butcher.
John Toby „ tanner,
together with others, &c.

Thomas Colbrond, of *Wortling*, gentilman.
Richard de Lay, of same, draper.
John Barward, of *Warbulton*, yoman.
William Peggan, of same, yoman.
John Jamyn „ husbondman.
Richard Wellis ,, carpenter.
Richard Brette, of *Eshpernham*, yoman.
Richard Ladde, of same, husbondman.
William Write, of *Nortlyng*, yoman.
Thomas Bricksnode, of same, yoman.
Thomas Austyn „ clerk.
John Pynfowle „ mercer.
John Brownfeld, of *Herst*, husbondman.
Peter Elys, of same, carpenter.
John Hamonde ,, fuller.
John Laude „ corveser.
William atte Stokke,, turner.
John Prat „ laborer.

[1] M. 8.

Alan Tysherst, of *Ashburnham*, carpenter,
Thomas Bole, of same, carpenter.
John Russell „
John Lampain, of *Wratlyng*, junior, butcher.
Thomas Burgeys, of same, husbondman.
John Whyte „ husbondman.

Richard Carpenter, *Balliff of Seford*,[2] yoman.
John Walkelyn „ junior, yoman.
Thomas Man ,, yoman.
John Crowelinke ,, yoman.
Simon Bernevale „ yoman.
John Chukke ,, yoman.
Robert Sampson „ yoman.
Richard Frensbe ,, yoman.
Thomas Barbour „ barber.
John Tanner ,, husbondman.
John Bocher „ butcher, and
all others of the same TOWN.

John Rakle, of *Willingdon*, gentilman.
John Bray, of *West Den*, senior, gentilman.
William Bray , gentilman.
John Parke(r), of *Willyngdon*, gentilman.

Symon Potteman, of *Fryston*, yoman, and
Thomas Hasilwode, of *Alfriston*, yoman, constables of the HUNDRED of ALSTONE.

Richard Seger, late of Alfriston, yoman, otherwise called Richard Seger, of *Marsfeld*, yoman.
Thomas Chapman, of *Alfriston*, chapman.
John Coptrowe ,, yoman.
Roger Trenshede ,, yoman.
Richard Chukke ,, baker.

[2] M. 7.

JOHN CADE'S FOLLOWERS IN SUSSEX. 81

Thomas Colyn, of *Alfriston*, yoman.
John Irland   ,,   yoman.
John Haweden   ,,   carpenter.
John Ray   ,,   junior,
  husbondman.
John Smyth   ,,   chapman.
William atte Dene   ,,   smith.
Edward atte Broke   ,,   husband-
  man.
Roger Smyth   ,,   smith.
Thomas Man   ,,   husbond-
  man.
Thomas Peckham   ,,   corveser.
John Hickes   ,,   smith.
John Colvile   ,,   junior,
  laborer.
John Benet   ,,   laborer.
John Crop   ,,   corveser.
Richard Profot, of *Milton*, yoman.
John Profot   ,,   husbondman.
Peter Profot   ,,   husbondman.
Robert Profot   ,,   husbondman.
Edward Newe   ,,   laborer;
and all and singular the men of the
  TOWNS aforesaid.

John Roser, of *Estlyng* (Guestling),
  and all other men within the HUN-
  DRED.

William Mason, of *Hastinges*, mason.
William Wytton, of same, dyer.
John Bychet   ,,   carpenter.
John Mayhewe   ,,   yoman.
Richard Hughson   ,,   yoman.
James Lok   ,,   helyar.
John Adam   ,,   syngleman.
Robert Knight   ,,   tailor.
John Clypsam   ,,   carpenter.
Osbert Watte   ,,   husbondman,.
  and
Edmund Letherland   ,,   yoman, &c.

John Lounsford, of *Battle*, gentilman.
Richard de Neve   ,,   laborer.
William atte Held   ,,   laborer.
John Ideyn   ,,   laborer.
John Fermesham   ,,   laborer.

Simon Martyn, of *Asheburnham*, laborer
William Martyn, of *Battle*, laborer.
Thomas Colyn, of *Asheburnham*, la-
  borer.
William Byrchet, of *Cattisfeld*, laborer·
John Byrchet   ,,   laborer.

John Hylder, of *Kingston juxta Lewes*,
  yoman, and
Richard Elyot, of *Smythwieke*, husbond-
  man, constables of the HUNDRED of
  SWANBERG.
Thomas Holybon, of *Iford*, senior, la-
  borer.
John Holybon,   ,,   husbondman.
William Holybon, of the *Cliff, near
  Lewes*, yoman.
John Machyn, of *Iford*, husbondman.
John Holybon, junior ,, laborer.
Simon Holybon   ,,   laborer.
Richard Sowedan, of *Westoute juxta
  Lewes*, webbe.
Thomas Hyches   ,,   carpenter.
William Merston   ,,   tailor;
together with many others of the
  HUNDRED aforesaid.

William Forger, of *Westfyrle*, yoman,
  with many others.

Thomas Styler, of *Rowesparr*, gentil-
  man.
Walter Styler   ,,   gentilman.
Thomas Styler   ,,   junior, gentil-
  man.
Thomas Bartelot   ,,   gentilman.
Thomas Horle   ,,   yoman.
John Frencham   ,,   husbondman.
Thomas Mose   ,,   husbondman.
John Tylth   ,,   husbondman.
Richard Gardyner   ,,   husbondman.
John Man   ,,   husbondman.
William Frenshe   ,,   husbondman.
William Gerad   ,,   husbondman.
Thomas Brode   ,,   husbondman.
Richard Hasty   ,,   laborer.
John Mose   ,,   husbondman.

M

82   JOHN CADE'S FOLLOWERS IN SUSSEX.

Richard Mose, of Rowesparr, husbondman, together with many others.

John atte Wythe, *Lamporte*, husbondman, and Thomas Underwood, of *Newyke*, yoman, constables of the HUNDRED of BERCOMBE.

Richard Profyt, of *Hammesay*, gentilman.
John Marqnyk   „   yoman.
Richard Marquyk   „   yoman.
Richard Blome   „   yoman.
Richard Hawkyn   „   yoman.
Thomas Trusloue   „   yoman.
Henry Perys, of *Bercompe*, yoman.
Thomas Sander   „   laborer.

John Parker, of *Hoo*,[1] yoman, constable of the HUNDRED of HOO.
John de Wellys,
Thomas de Brooke,
John Knelles,
William Scotte, of the HUNDRED aforesaid, and
John Broke, &c.

Roger Lacche, of *Litlyngton*, gentilman.
Henry atte Fonell   „   yoman.
John atte Fenell   „   husbondman.
Laurence atte Fenell   „   husbondman.
John Lyon   „   husbondman.
John Cheseman   „   husbondman.
Robert Parker   „   husbondman.

Thomas Profot, of *Estbourne*, gentilman.
Richard Burton   „   yoman.
Thomas Motard   „   yoman.

Gilbert Homewode, of *Cokefeld*, yoman, and
John Homewode, of *Plumpton*, yoman, constables of the HUNDRED of STREETEM.

John Wyldegoos, of *Holdelegh*, yoman.
John atte Roe, of *Wyvelysfeld* yoman.
Thomas Esthanfeld   „   yoman.

John Stempe, of *Suthuover, juxta Lewes*, constable of SOUTHOVER, near LEWES.

William Delve, of *Suthuover*, yoman.
Thomas Best   „   yoman.
Richard Dymmok   „   yoman.
Peter Bromfeld   „   yoman.
William Reymys   „   husbondman.
Richard Codnore   „   cooper.

Richard [Dertmouth], Abbot of St. MARTIN'S MONASTERY, of BATTLE, in the county of Sussex, and the Convent of the same place, and the servants of the said Abbot and Convent, &c.

Thomas Weston, of *Mafeld*.
Thomas   „   chaplain.
Thomas Harnes   „
John Hoke   „
John atte Ford   „
John Nevyll   „

The following is a copy of the pardon:—

D. pardonacōne Mortymer. { R. omnibus Ballivis et fidelibus suis ad quos, &c. sal't'm. Licet quidem Joh'es Mortymer simul cum alijs nonnullis in non modico set eximio et grandi numero in varijs et diversis locis regni n'ri presertim in com' Kanc' et locis adjacentibus et convicinis absq; mandato vel auctoritate n'ra sua propria temeritate ac presumpcōe se nup' congregand' et coadjuvand' duxerint adversus et contra leges, &c. &c. per presentes pardonamus, remittimus et relaxamus p^efato Joh'i ceterisq; omnibus et singulis secum ut premittitur associatis, congregatis, &c. &c.

T. R. apud Westmonast, vj die Julii.

[1] M. 4.

APPENDIX.*

Mr. Francis Bacon to the Lord Mayor (Sir James Pemberton).†

My very good Lord,—I did little expect, when I left yor Lordshipp last, that there woulde have bene a proceedinge against Mr Barnard to his overthrowe, of which I must confesse myself to have bene some cause, forasmuch as, hee relyinge upon me for counsel, I advised that course which hee followed. Wherein I begyn nowe to question with my self, whether in preferring my respects unto your Lp. and the rest, I have not failed in dutie of my profession towardes my client, ffor certenlie if the words had bene heynous, and spoken in a malitious fashion, and in some publique place, and well proved, and not a pratle in a taverne, caught hould of by one whoe (as I heare since) is not better than a knight of the post (Standish I meane), yet I know not what coulde have bene done more than to impose upon him a greevious fine, and to require the payment of ye same, and to take awaie his means of life by his disfranchisement, and to comitt him to a defamed prison during Christmas, in honor whereof the prisoners in doe com'onlie of grace obtaine some inlargement. This height of proceedinge, to tell your Lordshipp and the rest, as my good friendes, my opynion plainly, tendeth not to strengthen aucthoritie, which is best supported by love and feare, but rather to make people discontented and servile, especiallie when such punishment is inflicted for wordes not by any rule of lawe, but by a jurisdiction of discretion which would evermore be moderatelie (used). And I praie God, where Mr. Recorder did well and wiselie put you in minde of the admonitions you often receave from my Lordes,‡ that you bridle unrulie

Mr. Francis Bacon to my Lord Maior in reproach of the proceedings used against Mr. Barnard for Words.

* From the collection of copies of Letters in the Guildhall of London.
† Sir James Pemberton, a Goldsmith, born in Lancashire, Alderman of Bishopsgate.
‡ Lords of the Council.

tongues, that those kinde of speeches (whereunto those admonitions doe referr) which are concerninge the State and honor thereof doe not passe too licenciouslie in the Cittie unpunished, while those wordes which concerne your particuler are soe straightlie enquired into, and punished wth such extremitie. But these thinges your owne wisdomes, first or last, will best represent unto you; my writinge unto you at this time is to the end that, howsoever I doe take it somewhat unkindlie that my mediation prevailed noe more, yet I mought preserve that further respect that I am willinge to use unto such a state in deliveringe my opinion unto you freelie before I would be of counsell or move anie thinge that should crosse yor proceedinges. And though I be against you in this particuler, I shall contynewe neverthelesse in other thinges my wonted good affection to yourselves and yor busines. Grayes Inne, xxvijth December, 1611.

Yo^r verie lovyng frinde,
Fr. Bacon.

Sir Francis Bacon and Sir Henry Yelverton to the Lord Mayor (Sir Thomas Midleton).

Sir Frauncis Bacon to the Lorde Maior and Aldermenn to send some persons instructed to attend him and the King's Solicitor in the difference concerning the Bailwick of Oswalstone.

After our hartie comendations to yor good Lordshipp, whereas a petition hath bene exhibited to the King's Maiestie, intituling his Highness to the Baylywick of Oswalton in the countie of Midd. The graunte whereof the Lord Maior and Courte of Aldermen for the time beinge have of late made clayme unto, and forasmuch as it hath pleased his Maiestie to refer the consideration thereof unto us his Attorney and Solicito^r-General, Wee doe, by virtue thereof, and in his Ma^{ts} name, require yor Lpp and the Courte of Aldermen your bretheren, to send some sufficientlie instructed on yor behalf to the chamber of me, his Maiesties Attorney-Generall, at Graies Inn, on the fower and twentieth daie of this instant moneth of Marche, at two of the clock in the afternoone, to shewe unto us by what title or interest you claime the same, whereof wee desire you not to faile. Thus much wee did signifie formerlie to yor Lpp in forme of an open l're or warrant. And wee would have y^r Lordshipp to knowe that it was noe erro^r nor defect of forme soe to doe in a cause referred unto us from his Maiestie, and wherein you onlie required to attend by counsell and not otherwise in person. But because wee will not differ upon ceremonies with your Lorshipp that wee love so well, wee have fitted this forme to yor owne desire, and soe wee bid you hartelie farewell.

Yo^r Lp^s lovinge frindes,
Fr. Bacon, Henry Yelverton.

Grayes Inne, this xxijth of March, 1613.

To the Right Honorable Sr Thomas Midleton,* Knighte,
Lord Maior of the Cittie of London.

Sir Francis Bacon to the Lord Mayor (Sir Thomas Midleton.)

After my hartie commendac'ons to yor Lordshipp. The cause concerninge the Bayliwick Oswaldston (wherewith yor L'pp by my former letters hath bene made acquainted) was debated before mee the other dai for the Kinge, and for the cittie, whereby I finde (howsoever the right fall out, for the Kinge, or cittie, which is verie questionable). That the Sheriffs have not the power of disposinge thereof neither by the Charter of the cittie, nor by construction of the lawe, beinge Sheriffes by Charter of two counties and but a member of this corporation to which the graunte of the countie of Midd' is made; besides the Sheriffes are by lawe removeable at the will of the Lord Maior and cominaltie, and by theire owne consents, by Acts of Com'on counsell, by severall orders in your L'p's courte, the Sheriffes are not to dispose thereof, soe as the question is onelie (as in former times I find it hath bene) betweene the King and your L'pp. (Whether the Kinge or the Courte of Lord Maior and Aldermen is interessed therein.) Wherein out of my respecte to your L'p and the Citie, and for the avoidinge of contention and charge, I would wish that Mr. Owen might enioye the same for his life, procuring to the cittie for ever from his Maiestie his Highness righte thereunto. And I doe the rather advise it because his Ma^{ty} havinge by waye of recomendation

Sr Frauncis Bacon to my Lord Maior to have Mr. Owen to be Bailie of Oswalstone for his life, and to cease contention, shewinge his opynion concerning the righte of bestowing the said office.

---

* Sir Thomas Midleton, M.P. for London, brother to Sir Hugh, who had a goldsmith's shop in Basinghall Street, much frequented by Sir Walter Raleigh. Sir Thomas was a Grocer. The New River was opened during his mayoralty. Alderman of Queenhithe. Was committed to Newgate before he would accept office. James the First tried to get his own favourites exempted from public service, but in this case without success. The City insisted that their chief citizens should discharge City duties.

written in the behalf of the said Mr. Owen (not soe much standinge uppon his righte as out of a gratious favoure unto the Cittie) and his Ma^{ts} predecessors having often obtayned the same to avoide strife, It might be construed that his Maiestie my Maister hath either lesse regard from the Cittie, or lesse righte than his progenitors, which I would be loth should in either kinde be thoughte. And this is the effect of that I wished Mr. Stone to deliver to y^r Lpp. As for his Ma^{ts} righte, if it come to that, I am bounde to mayntaine it and will. And soe I bidd your L'pp verie hartelie farewell. From Greyes Inne the xxvjth of June, 1614.

Yo^r Lp^s verie loving frinde,
Fr. Bacon.

To the Right Honorable Sr Thomas Midleton, Knight,
Lord Maior of the Cittie of London.

Sir Francis Bacon to the Lord Mayor.

After my verie harty comendac'ons to y^r Lp and your bretheren, whereas the honor and strength of the Citty in all ages hath been greately supported by the learned of the same, who, for their learning and integritie, have bin recomended to y^r predecessors by such as could iudge of the worthes and abilities in that behalfe, wch they very gravely and providently have ordeyned, that those learned men should succeed such as were the hono^{ble} Councill of the Cittie, and in the meane tyme to encourage them to take paines to instruct themselves in the lawes and customes of the Citty, have made choice of them to be of the Councell at lardge, alloweinge them a small yerely fee to oblige them to that Cittie, wch course being soe hono^{ble} and beneficiall to the Citty and soe agreeable with your laudable customes, I wish may still be continued. And albeit I have not hitherto recomended any to you in this nature, yet this bearer, Mr. Thomas Brickenden, being not only in my opinion, but in the opinion likewise of the whole bench of Grayes Inne, where he liveth, for his religion, learninge, and integritie, a gentleman verie fitt to doe the Citty service in that kinde, I have thought fitt to recommende him vnto you, praying you for my sake to accepte of him, and to graunte that he may succede in the place of one of your foure pleaders next after one Mr. Salter, to whome, as I understande, the like graunt in revercion hath bin lately made by the Lord Maior for the tyme being and his brethren; the which your kindness and loving performance I shall take as a speciall curtesie, and will both remember and requite the same whensoever you shall have occasion to use mee. And soe I rest,

Ever your assured loving frende,

Ffr. Bacon.

Sir Francis Bacon to the Lord Mayor.

After my verie heartie comendac'ons to your Lo'ps : Whereas I doe vnderstande that the late Lorde Chauncelor had by your curtesie and suffrance the comoditie of water for his house conveyed by a pipe of leade to Yorke house out of the mayne pipe that serveth the Cittie of London w^h water, my householde being speedily to settle and reside at Yorke house I desier the like respecte of you, that I may haue the necessarie use of water for my house, and I shalbe ready to acknowledge your kindness herein. Soe I bid your Lo'p verie hartie far well. Whitehall, July 25, 1617.

Y^r Lops verie loving frend,

F. Bacon.

To the Right Honble Sir John Lemon,[*] Knighte,
Lord Maior of the Cittie of London, and the
Aldermen his brethren be these.

Lord Bacon to the Lord Mayor.

After my verie harty comendations to your Ldps: Whereas there is a commission lately issued under the great seale for collection of moneys within the Citties of London and Westminster and divers other Shires, For the more speedie repairing and building of Stainse Bridge and Egham Causeway, and for that purpose, respecting the case as extraordinary, the churchwardens and petty constables are to make these collections at the houses of the inhabitants, and to endorse the names of those that shall contribute towards the same upon the brifet, and to retourne the same wth their collections to such Justices of Peace as the Judges of Assise shall appointe in every county, who are

[*] Sir John Lemon. A Fishmonger. From Norfolk. Alderman of Langbourn. President of Christ's Hospital.

88   APPENDIX.

likewise to retourne the money soe collected to the bridgmasters of Stanes by the end of Easter terme nexte. I haue therefore thought good, in regard of the present necessitie of the wourke, as well for the conveniency of his Matie carriage over the said bridge and causeways, as alsoe for the greate ease of all the subiects that travell to and from London for the Westerne part, to write these my letters unto you, praying your care in the furtherance of the said collec'on within the Citty of London, and for the nominating of such Aldermen to whom the saide shalbee paid unto by the churchwardens and constables, to be delivered over by them to the said bridgemasters of Stanes accordingly. So I bidde your l'ps verie hartily farwell. From Yorke house, this 20th of February 1618.

Yr lo'ps verie loving frend,
F. VERULAM.

To the Right hon^{ble} his very good lord the Lord
  Maior of London,* and to his verie loving
  frendes the Aldermen his brethren.

LORD BACON AND OTHERS TO THE LORD MAYOR.

After my verie hartie comendacons to your Lop, being moved on the behalfe of this gentleman, Mr. Edward Ayscough, a barrester of Graye Inne, one of good and honest conversation, and well deserving, I have thought good by these my l'res to recommend him to your Lo'ps favour, hartily praying you to graunte him the reverc'on of one of the places of the Councell of the Citty wch you terme Com'on Pleaders in the Citty, wch I doubt not but hee will soe well performe as you shell thinke it worthyly bestowed on him, and myselfe shall take it as a kindnes done the rather for my sake. Soe I bid your Lo'p verie hartily farwell. From Yorke house, the 21st of November, 1620.

Your Lo'ps very loving frend,
F. VERULAM CANC.

To the Right Hono^{ble} Sir Frauncis Jones,† Knight,
  Lord Maior of the City of London, and the
  rest of the Aldermen, his brethren.

---

* Sir Sebastian Harvey. His father was Lord Mayor in 1581. Alderman of Cheap. An Ironmonger.

† Haberdasher. Alderman of Aldgate. From Shropshire. Was he related to his contemporary, Alderman Sir Roger Jones, the ancestor of Lord Ranelagh?

APPENDIX.

LORD BACON AND OTHERS TO THE LORD MAYOR.

After our very hartie comendac'ons to your Lo'p and the rest, whereas we are informed that by the preferment of Mr. Coventry to the office of Recorder of London, his late office of Judge of one of the Sheriffs Courts is become voyde and fallen to Mr. Richard Gippes, who hath a graunte in reverc'on of the same, ffor as much as neither the said Mr. Gippes nor his sufficiencie and abilitie to discharge that place can be soe well knowne to you as to us, we have thought fitt to testifie our knowledge of him, that is, that he is an utter barrester of this howse of good continu[ance] and learned and discrete, and every way [able] to performe the dutie of that place, and recommend him and his suite to your Lo^p and the rest. Wee bid you hartily farewell. Grays Inne, this 20th November, 1626.

Your Lo$^{p's}$ very loving friends,

FR. BACON, HY. YELVERTON,
ED. MOSELY, THO. TILDESLEY,
NICOLAS FFULKE, GEOFREY
NIGHTINGALE, FRA. DEEKIN,
HUMPERY DAVENPORT, JAMES
MAYNE.

To the R^t Hono^{ble} the Lord Maior * of the
Cittie of London, and the Right Wor.
the Aldermen of the same.

* Sir Cuthbert Hacket, Draper. From Dartford. Alderman of Portsoken.

SIR RALPH JOCELYN.

Sir Ralph Jocelyn, K.B. citizen and draper, was the son of Geoffry Jocelyn, of Sawbridgeworth. His first wife was Philippa, daughter and coheiress of alderman Philip Malpas. He was Sheriff of London in 1458, Mayor in 1464, and again in 1476. Sir Ralph Jocelyn was made a Knight of the Bath at the coronation of Queen Elizabeth, the consort of Edward the Fourth, in the year 1465, together with his brother-in-law Sir Thomas Cooke (mayor 1462), Sir Matthew Philipp (mayor 1463), and Sir Henry Weever (sheriff 1465). He was M.P. for London, and executor to the will of his father-in-law Philip Malpas.[1] He was a careful corrector of the malpractices of bakers and victuallers in the city of London, and by his diligence the walls of the city were repaired. He died in 1478, and was buried at St. Swithin's London Stone.[2] His portrait and that of his second wife Elizabeth (daughter and heiress to William Berkley[3]) is in one of the windows of Melford church, Suffolk. It was also at Aspeden church, Hertfordshire; and H. Chapman, in his Survey of Aspeden Church, published in 1783, mentions having fortunately made a note of this portrait in the chancel window on his first visit to the church, for on going there again a few days after he found the glass broken, but succeeded in recovering—from the wreck outside— the head unbroken, and made an accurate drawing of it, an engraving of which accompanies the Survey, of which the annexed Plate is a fac-simile; he also states that underneath was the inscription—

pro bono statu Radulphi Jossil.

No record is to be found in the corporation archives of his election as an alderman.

From an Inquisition post mortem taken at Bekynsfeld, in the county

---

[1] See page 7.
[2] See Weever's *Funerall Monuments*, 1631.
[3] *The Beauties of England and Wales*, vol. vii. p. 194.

Syr Raufe Jocelyn.

APPENDIX.   91

of Buckingham, 2nd Nov. A.D. 1478, 18 Edw. IV.[1] it appears that by virtue of a certain feoffment Sir Ralph Jocelyn was with others seized of the manors of Lynchelade and Southcote in that county, and that he died on the 12th of October then last past, and that the said manors were valued beyond reprisals at 10 marks.

From another Inquisition post mortem taken at Stratford Langthorn, in the county of Essex, on Thursday next after the feast of All Saints, A.D. 1478, 18 Edw. IV. it appears that Philip Malpas, citizen and alderman of London, was seized in fee of the manor of Chaldewell, and of certain lands with appurtenances lying in the parish of Westham, and, being so seized, by his charter demised the said manor and lands to the said Ralph Jocelyn and Philippa then his wife for the term of their lives and the life of the longest liver of them, and after their deaths the said manor and lands to remain to Elizabeth late wife of Thomas Cooke, knt., daughter of the said Philip Malpas, and her heirs for ever. The said manor was valued at 40 marks per annum beyond reprisals, and the lands at 40 shillings per annum. This Inquisition also sets forth that Sir Ralph Jocelyn died on Monday next after the feast of Saint Edward the King and Martyr last past, without heirs of his body, and that George Jocelyn his nephew (son of his brother Thomas Jocelyn,) was found to be his next heir and of the age of fifty years and more.

Another Inquisition post mortem was taken at Waltham Cross, in the county of Hertford, on Thursday next after the feast of All Saints, A.D. 1478, 18 Edw. IV., from which we glean, that, before the death of Sir Ralph, Christopher Chadwyll clerk, rector of the church of Aspeden, and Roger Morice of the same yeoman, being seized in fee of the manor of Aspeden Hall, in Aspeden aforesaid, and of certain lands and tenements situate in the parishes of Buntingford, Layston, Throcking, Widdial, Wakely, and Westmill, in the county of Hertford, by their charter, dated at Aspeden, 4th April, A.D. 1478, 18 Edw. IV. did demise the same unto Sir Ralph Jocelyn and Elizabeth his wife, for the term of their lives, and after their decease to remain to John Say, knight, (who is stated to have since deceased,) William Barke, and John Clopton esquires, Thomas Rygby, Robert Molyneux, William Dunthorn gentlemen, William Bulstrede, Robert Godewyn pannar', and Henry Wodecok, and their heirs and assigns for ever, which is stated to fully appear by the last will of Sir Ralph as well as by

[1] Inq. post mortem, No. 28, 18 Edw. IV.

the said charter. Sir Ralph died seized of the said lands by virtue of this demise, and his wife Elizabeth survived him [1] and was solely seized of the same; and the said manor was valued at 20 marks per annum beyond all reprisals, and the lands at 40 shillings per annum. This Inquisition also sets forth that Sir Ralph died without heirs of his body, and that George Jocelyn, his nephew, was found to be his next heir.[2]

It is evident from the information afforded by these inquisitions that the family of Earl Roden does not descend from Sir Ralph Jocelyn. It is also evident that he did not die intestate; but, although a careful search has been made for his will, it has been without success.

For my burial, I desire it may be in St. Michael's Church, St. Alban's; THERE WAS MY MOTHER BURIED, and it is the parish church of my mansion house of Gorhambury, and it is the only Christen church within the walls of old Verulam.—*Lord Bacon's Will.*

ARMS OF BACON.

IN THE NORTH WINDOW OF THE CHANCEL OF ST. MICHAEL'S CHURCH, ST. ALBAN'S.

Quarterly: first and third, Gules, on a chief argent two mullets sable, *Bacon.* Second and fourth, Or, three bars azure, over all a bend of the same voided gules, *Quaplode.* A crescent for difference.

Impaling: quarterly, 1. Or, a chevron compony gules and azure between three cinquefoils of the last, *Cooke.* 2. Sable, a fesse between three pheons argent, *Malpas.* 3. Azure, three eagles displayed in bend cotised argent, *Belknap.* 4. Or, an eagle displayed with two heads sable charged with a fleur-de-lis argent, *Kirhile* (?) 5. Gules, a fesse chequy argent and sable between six crosses formée fitchée argent, *Boteler.* 6. Or, two bends gules, *Sudeley* 7. Bendy of ten or and azure, *Montfort* or *Montford.*

These arms—which are delineated in the accompanying plate—were removed from Gorhambury some years since and fixed in the north window of the chancel of St. Michael's church, by order, it is said,

---

[1] She married secondly Sir Robert Clifford (third son of Lord Clifford), who held the manor of Aspeden in her right; he was one of those implicated in the Perkin Warbeck conspiracy.

[2] Our pedigree is therefore wrong. The reader is requested to correct it accordingly.

ARMS IN THE NORTH WINDOW OF CHANCEL
OF S? MICHAELS CHURCH, S? ALBANS.

These arms were taken out of a window at Gorhambury
and placed in the window of chancel a few years since,
by order of Lord Verulam.

of Lord Verulam. They prove an interesting evidence of the alliance of the *Bacon* and *Cooke* families.

A similar impalement occurs on the Hoby arms in Bisham church, Suffolk, on the monument of Sir Thomas Hoby, with the exception that the arms of *Kirhile* (?) are shown in the third quartering and those of *Belknap* in the fourth.[1]

LORD BACON.

He was understood by some. Ben Jonson, after the author's death, described the book in terms of the highest praise: "Though by most of superficial men, who cannot get beyond the title of nominals, it is not penetrated nor understood, it really openeth all defects of learning whatsoever. My conceit of his person was never increased towards him by his place or honours. But I have and do reverence him for the greatness that was only proper in himself, and in that he seemed to me ever by his work one of the greatest men and most worthy of admiration that had been in many ages." The King, although he had expressed what doubtless he felt, the difficulty of understanding the work, wrote to Bacon, stating that he agreed with him in many of his remarks, and assured him that he could not have "made choice of a subject more befitting his place and his universal and methodical knowledge." Sir Henry Wotton, on receiving three copies, expressed himself thus :—" Your lordship hath done a great and everliving benefit to all the children of nature, and to nature herself in her uppermost extent of latitude, who never before had so noble nor so true an interpreter, never so inward a secretary of her cabinet." On the continent the work was more highly honoured than at home, being esteemed by many of the most competent judges as one of the most important accessions ever made to philosophy.—*Engl. Enc. Biog.*, vol. i. p. 473.

[1] Add. MS. Brit. Mus. No. 19,124, f. 241.

ILLUSTRATIONS OF THE CLOSE CONNECTION OF LORD BACON WITH THE CORPORATION OF LONDON, TAKEN FROM THE GUILDHALL RECORDS.

> But now behold,
> In the quick forge and working house of thought,
> How London doth pour out her citizens!
> The Mayor and all his brethren *in best sort*,—
> Like to the senators of the antique Rome.—*Shakespeare.*

Lady Bacon's father was Benedict Barnham, draper, elected Alderman of Bread Street Ward, 1591.

Lady Bacon's grandfather, Francis Barnham, draper, elected Alderman of Farringdon Without, 19th December, 1568.

Lord Bacon's uncle, James Bacon, fishmonger (also a mercer), elected Alderman of Aldersgate Ward, 22nd April, 1567.

Lord Bacon's grandfather, William Fitzwilliam, (ancestor of Earl Fitzwilliam,) citizen and tailor, elected Alderman of Bread Street Ward, 7th November, 1505; made a Privy Councillor by Henry VIII.; a new Alderman chosen in his place 15th May, 1510.

Lord Bacon's great-grandfather, Sir John Hawes, Alderman and Sheriff, 1500.

Lord Bacon's uncle's father-in-law, John Cawnton, haberdasher, elected Alderman of Bishopsgate, 6th October, 1523.

Lord Bacon's great-great-great-grandfather, Sir Thomas Cooke, K.B., draper, JACK CADE'S LONDON AGENT, elected Alderman of Vintry Ward, 4th October, 1457.

Lord Bacon's great-great-great-great-grandfather, Philip Malpas, draper and mercer, M.P. for London, elected Alderman of Lime Street Ward, 1st April, 1447.

SIR ANTHONY COOKE.

Sir Anthony Cooke was born at Gidea Hall, in Essex. He was a man eminent in all the circles of the arts, preferring contemplation to active life, and skilled in education. "Contemplation," says Lloyd, "was his soul, privacy his life, and discourse his element. Business was his purgatory, and publicity his torment. He took more pleasure to breed up statesmen than to be one. He managed his family and children with such prudence and discretion, that Lord Seymour, standing by one day when this gentleman chid his son, said '*Some men govern families with more skill than others do kingdoms*,' and thereupon commended him to the government of his nephew, Edward VI. Such the majestie of his looks and gate, that awe governed; such the reason and sweetness, that love obliged all his family—a family equally afraid to displease so *good* a head, and to offend so *great*. In their marriage they were guided by his reason, more than by his will; and rather *directed* by his counsel, than *led* by his authority."

He had five daughters, whose education he superintended; and, thinking that women are as capable of learning as men, he instilled that to his daughters at night, what he had taught the Prince in the day; and all the daughters of Sir Anthony Cooke were perfectly skilled in the learned languages, which is apparent from his bequest of Latin and Greek books to each of them. They married suitably to the education with which they had been formed.

MILDRED COOKE, LADY BURGHLEY.

By Lord Burghley.[1]

"About   yeres sence, she caused exhibitions to be secretly given by the hands of the master of St. Jhons in Cambridg for the mayntenance of two scholars. For a perpetuitie whereof to contynew, she did cause some lands to be purchased in the name of the Dean of Westmynster, who also did assure the same to that colledg for a perpetuall mayntenance of the said two scholars in that colledg. All which was done without any signification of hir act or charg to any manner of person but only of the Deane, and one William Walter of Wymbleton, whose advise was used for the wrytyng of the purchase and assurance.

"She did also, with the privite of Mr. Deanes of Powles and Westmynstre, and of Mr. Aldersy, beyng fre of the Haberdashers in London, give to the Company of the sayd Haberdashers a good some of money; whereby is provyded that every two yers there is lent to six poore men of certen speciall occupations, as smyths, carpyntors,

---

[1] From the *Biographica Britannica*, vol. iv. p. 96.

weavors, and such like in Romford in Essex, twenty pounds a pece, in the whole one hundred and twenty pounds. And in Chesthunt and Wooltham to other six lik persons twenty marks a pece, in the whole four-score pound. Which releff by way of loan is to continew. By the same means is provided for twenty poore people in Chesthunt, the first sonday of every month, a meass of meate, in flesh, bread, and money for drynk. And lykwise is provided four marks yerly for four sermons to be preached quarterly, by one of the preachers of Jhon's Colledg. And these distributions have been made a long time, whylest she lyved, by some of my servants, without gyvyng me knqwledg therof; though indede, I had cause to thynk that she did sometymes bestow such kynd of alms, but not that I knew of any order taken for contynuaunce thereof; for she wold rather co'enly use speches with me, how she was disposed to give all that she cold to some such uses if she cold devise to have the same faythfully performed after hir liff; wherof she alwayes pretended many doubts. And for that she used the advise of Mr. Deanes of Powles and of Westmynster, and wold have her actions kept secrett, she forced upon them some small peces of plate to be used in their chambres, as remembrances of hir good will for their paynes.

"She did also four tymes in the yere secretly send to all the prisons of London money to buy bread, chese, and drink co'enly for four hundred persons, and many times more, without knolledg from whom the same come.

"She did lykwise sondry tymes send shyrts and smokks to the poore people, both in London and at Chesthunt.

"She also gave a some of money to the master of St. Jhon's Colledg to procure to have fyres in the hall of that colledg upon all sondays and hollydayes betwixt the fest of All Sayntes and Candelmas, whan ther war no ordinary fyres of the charge of the colledg.

"She gave also a sume of mony secretly towards a buyldyng for a new waye at Cambridg to the Co'en Scolles.

"She also provyded a great nomber of books, whereof she gave some to the University of Cambridge, namely, the great Bible in Hebrew and four other tongs. And to the Colledge of Saint John's very many books in Greke, of divinite and physick, and of other sciences. The lyk she did to Christ's Chyrch and St. John's Colledg in Oxford. The lyk she did to the Colledg of Westminster.

"She did also yerly provyde wooll and flaxe, and did distribute it to women in Chesthunt parish, wyllyng them to work the same into yarn, and to bryng it to hir to se ther manner of workying; and for the most part she gave to them the stuff by way of alms. Some tyme she caused the same to be wrought into cloth and gave it to the poore, paying first for the spynning more than it was worth.

"Not long afor hir deth, she caused secretly to be bought a large quantite of wheat and rye to be disposed amongst the poore in tyme of derth. Which remained unspent at the time of hir deth; but the same confessed by such as provyded it secretly. And therfor in conscience to be so distributed accordyng to hir mynd. April 9th, 1589. Written at Collings Lodge by me in sorrow. W. B."

LADY BACON.

Ana, the second daughter of Sir Anthony Cooke, was born in 1528. She had the same liberal education which was bestowed upon her elder sister, and perhaps under the same tutor. Having added much acquired knowledge to great natural endowments, she made an illustrious figure among the literati of that period; and hence acquired so extraordinary a reputation, that she is said to have been constituted governess to King Edward the Sixth. If this be a fact, it is a very surprising one, since she could not be much more than twenty-five years of age at the death of that young monarch, and only nineteen years old when he began to reign. However that matter may stand, it is certain that she early became eminent for piety, virtue, and learning, and that she was skilled in the Greek, Latin, and Italian tongues. At what time she was married to Sir Nicholas Bacon has not been exactly ascertained. Her eldest son Anthony was born in 1558, and her youngest son Francis on the 22nd of January, 1560-61.—*Biogr. Brittan.* vol. iv. pp. 96–97.

Elizabeth Cooke, third daughter of Sir Anthony, born 1529, married, first, Sir Thomas Hoby. He was Ambassador to France of Queen Elizabeth: by him she had two sons and two daughters. The sons gave her uneasiness. She married, secondly, John Lord Russell, and their daughter Ann became the mother of the celebrated Marquis of Worcester, the author of *A Century of Inventions,* in which the steam-engine is first described. He was the father of the first Duke of Beaufort.

Katherine Cooke, fourth daughter of Sir Anthony, born in 1530, married Sir Henry Killigrew at St. Peter-le-Poer, London. She was buried in the church of St. Thomas Apostle, Vintry Ward, London. Her second daughter, Elizabeth, married Sir Jonathan Trelawny, and was the ancestress of the Bishop of that name, one of the SEVEN BISHOPS who opposed James the Second.

> "And shall Trelawny die brave boys, and shall Trelawny die?
> There's thirty thousand Cornishmen will know the reason why."

Margaret Cooke, the second wife of Sir Ralph Rowlett, died 1571, s. p., during her father's life. She was buried at St. Mary Staining, London.

The subjoined quotations from writers of different periods tell their own tale, as regards eminent Englishmen of the same blood, at various epochs of our history.

ALDERMAN SIR THOMAS COOKE, K.B.

"He was of the Commons' House, and therewith a man of great boldness of speech, and well spoken, and singularly witted and well reasoned."—*Fabyan.*

LORD BACON.

"There happened in my time one noble speaker who was full of quantity in his speaking: his language, where he could spare or pass by a jest, was richly censorious. No man ever spake more greatly, more purely, more weightily, or suffered less emptiness, less idleness in what he uttered; no member of his speech but what consisted of its own graces. His hearers could not cough, or look aside from him, without loss; he commanded when he spake, and had his judges angry and pleased at his devotion. No man had their affections more on his person; the fear of every man that heard him was lest he should make an end."—*Ben Jonson.*

APPENDIX. 99

MARQUIS OF SALISBURY.

"He has proved himself in the Commons an orator, an administrator, and it may be added, a thinker of the first class; and whereas others give promise at their first entrance into public life, too often falsified in later years, Lord Salisbury has developed a higher character by experience and familiarity with the problems of statesmanship. All were aware of his ability, but few could have anticipated the breadth of view he manifested during the short time in which he controlled the destinies of the Indian empire."—*The Times, April 14th, 1868.*

Monument in the Parish Church of St. Martin's-in-the-Fields
TO
THE WORTHY, LEARNED, AND GODLY GENTLEMAN,

WILLIAM COOKE, Esquire, her deare husband, sonne to the right worshippfull Sr Anthony Cooke knight, Frances his most loveing wife, daughter to that most noble gentleman the Lord John Gray, brother to the sometime high and mighty Prince Henry Gray the last Duke of Suffolke, hath dedicated this monument in memory of his virtue and her love, dyed the 14 day of May, and in the yeare of his age 56. Anno Dom' 1589.

> This Tombe for her Deare Spouse
> hath noble Francis plac'd,
> Lamenting much with greater guifts
> This Tombe should not be grac'd.
> And grieves as much companion-like
> This Tombe should not containe
> Theire wills in earth, since both on earth
> One will they did retaine.

Westminster: Printed by Nichols and Sons, 25, Parliament Street.

www.ingramcontent.com/pod-product-compliance
Lightning Source LLC
Chambersburg PA
CBHW022143160426
43197CB00009B/1405